SOLDIER SOLDIER

SOLDIER SOLDIER

Diary of a Soldier

Jonathan Guy Lewis

EBURY PRESS
LONDON

Dedication

To everyone that I worked with while making 'Soldier, Soldier' and also to my son Abraham.

First published in 1997

1 3 5 7 9 10 8 6 4 2

First published in the United Kingdom in 1997 by Ebury Press
Random House, 20 Vauxhall Bridge Road, London SW1V 2SA

Random House Australia (Pty) Limited
20 Alfred Street, Milsons Point, Sydney,
New South Wales 2061, Australia

Random House New Zealand Limited
18 Poland Road, Glenfield, Auckland 10, New Zealand

Random House South Africa (Pty) Limited
Endulini, 5a Jubilee Road, Parktown 2193, South Africa

Random House UK Limited Reg. No. 954009

Papers used by Ebury Press are natural, recyclable products made from wood grown in sustainable forests.

A CIP catalogue record for this book is available from the British Library.
ISBN 0 09 186340 6

Project editor Emma Callery
Designed by Jerry Goldie Graphic Design
Jacket designed by Blackjacks

Printed and bound in Portugal by Printer Portuguesa L.d.a.

PREVIOUS PAGE: The Boyzone Fusiliers on tour.

Contents

Introduction

At the beginning of November 1995, when my son Abraham was just three weeks old, my wife Miranda and I decided to take him to a wedding in South Wales. It was to be our first long weekend away as a family. We had to stop every half an hour or so for a breastfeeding session and during one of the homeward-bound enforced stops on the Monday, I decided to phone my friend Andy, for an update on his life. However, Andy's phone number is very similar to my agent's number, Denise, and without thinking, I suddenly found myself talking to her, listening to the fond enquiry, 'Where the hell are you?' I was supposed to be at a preliminary interview for the part of the new platoon sergeant in 'Soldier, Soldier'. I had written the interview down in my diary for the Tuesday, not the Monday.

This was one of those rare interviews where the character breakdown would suggest that your name was written all over it in huge capital letters. I had been the proud recipient of an army scholarship at school and I'd just had my first play – 'Our Boys', about my experiences as a patient in a military hospital – performed to some critical acclaim at the Donmar Warehouse theatre in London's West End.

This was not an auspicious start for a job that I really wanted, but fortunately Denise managed to rearrange the interview for a few days later. Annie Tricklebank (the producer) and Jane Arnell (casting) were lovely and things just seemed to click. We moved swiftly on to a second interview which went even better.

A few weeks later and I was in that zombie-like state between life and work: doing very serious praying to God, Satan, Allah and Krishna, and making several Samaritan-like phone calls to Denise, my hotline to the source, who was ever so good at calming me down. Lots of 'It's not the end of the world if you don't get it'-type reassurance. But then came the call: 'Jane says it's an offer – official.'

Getting the 'yes, the part's yours' phone call is always the best part of any acting job. I think most actors would agree, or at least shamefully admit, if you bribed them with a drink. It's a sad state of affairs, but I find that rarely does a job live up to the expectation. Looking back after two years with the series I think it's fair to say the experience has been more of a love-hate relationship. Living with the presence of 'Soldier, Soldier', with things changing from day to day, the pressure of getting things right quickly, has been hard. But the benefits and security of regular income from a regular acting job in a high profile TV series have far outweighed the negative aspects.

The series this year has, I think, changed direction. People said the same last year. Series VI was the first series post-Robson and Jerome. And in many quarters the expectation was, 'Oh, it'll never be the same without them', which of course is true. But, 'Oh, it'll never be as good', was just not the case. It was different. It had to be. Over the course of five series it had become increasingly about a couple of relationships. Even though the more discerning 'Soldier, Soldier' fans could tell you otherwise, I suspect the public at large's perception was of Robson Green and Jerome Flynn and Rosie Rowell and Holly Aird. It's the mark of a shrewd producer who's able to pull off a series without the principal actors, compete against the European football, and still average 10.5 million viewers per episode. The series last year was harder, more action, lots of new characters, and saw The King's Own going airborne. It returned to the style of the very first series.

My character, Chris, had transferred from the Paras due to a knee injury which left him unable to go on operational jumps and therefore no longer able to gain further promotion. He preferred to continue his career and promotion prospects by transferring to another front-line infantry battalion.

The series then saw Chris reunited with a son he never knew he had and a separation from wife Angela as he struggled to come to terms with this bolt out of the blue – working out whether he still held a torch for Liam's mother, Aoife, from whom he was suddenly parted after his CO in Northern Ireland found out about his secret relationship with a Catholic girl at about the same time as her family found out.

Parallel to this story was that of Jeremy Forsythe, with him embarking on a dangerous liaison with the CO's wife, Dr Sarah Eastwood. This story line received the most contentious mail over the whole series, especially from viewers with a military connection. We also had a war in the fictional South Atlantic Caravian Islands, which I think I nearly won single-handedly, and a wedding between Butcher (Danny Cunningham) and Stacey (the CO's driver).

At the start of this year, things at the King's Own Fusiliers are very different again. The feel of the series is more jokey and upbeat. The lads are getting up to no good in their personal lives and at work. Back for a second series is Fiona Bell who plays Sergeant Angela McCleod, Kate O'Malley, now Mrs, but still Private, Stacey Butcher and Corporal Mark Hobbs – played by Ian Curtis.

Ben Nealon has said that this year – his fourth – will be his last as Captain Jeremy Forsythe. And although I never like to say never, I think in Ben's case it's unlikely that Captain Forsythe is going to progress up the ladder to series 20 to become the CO of The King's Own. He says he's just grateful for the rarest of opportunities to take a character on a real journey from novice second lieutenant and a young Rupert straight out of Sandhurst (as Ben was straight out of drama school), to Company Commander, breaker of hearts.

Joining us this year are James Cosmo, who plays the tough new CO, Lt Col Drysdale, and Conor Mullen, the even tougher Company Sergeant Major that he brings in to sort out B Company. Tom Craig plays Fusilier Barton and Chris Gascoyne, Fusilier Rossi. They get most of the laughs, and Tom and Chris team up with Michelle Butterly as Julie Oldroyd for an involved and protracted love triangle which doesn't reach a climax until the very last episode.

I hope you all enjoy the course of the series and reading this diary as much as I have enjoyed keeping it. I have had particular fun marrying up the actors and crews with their ideal castings from the movies which you will find scattered throughout the book. It has given us all no end of amusement and occasionally helped to fill in the time when there has been a whole lot of sitting around. I know I'll look back with fond memories at this period in my personal and professional life, and at least my son will have some record of what his father was up to during the first few years of his life. Thank you.

Line of departure

Wednesday 5 February Episode 3

Picked up at 5.10am! The middle of the night. Here we go again.

Welcome to 'Soldier, Soldier'. Unfortunately, that's par for the course on a filming day. Anyway, think positive. Set Meals are doing the catering this year – a very important plus. As an army marches on its stomach, so does any film crew, and 'Soldier, Soldier' is no exception. Thankfully, Set Meals are one of the best location caterers in the business so I can lie back in the car and think of a poached egg and bacon sandwich on brown bread with dollops of HP sauce. And I think I've got it bad, but find out that Howard (ideal casting: a young Danny DeVito), my driver, was up at half-past three!

They've been filming for two days now (all interiors), so this will be the first day for everyone outside. When the sun finally does come up, it's a beautiful clear blue sky – fresh rather than cold. But I've got my Russian Army hat just in case. It's Siberian rabbit fur and fresh from the film I just did in Poland. Six pounds at the market in Warsaw, and even then I've been told I was ripped off. It's actually too warm for today. But Goddamit! I'm going to wear that hat if it kills me. 'This is Berkshire not the Baltic!', says Andy from the wardrobe department. 'You wait till 3am on a freezing February night shoot', I remind him. 'Why didn't you?', he retorts.

Why does Andy's brain always seem to have that sickening ability to work much faster than anyone else's? It's Andy's job to make sure we look the way we're supposed to look – in front of the camera, at least. He always has a tough job with us but somehow manages to keep us all in line, without ever losing his cool. How he does it, I do not know. It's nice to see Andy again. A familiar face from last year. He was always one hundred percent efficient and reliable, and a nice guy with it.

They're filming episode 3 first and we're not all that sure exactly what happens in episodes 1 and 2 other than a basic outline, and things can change at any time. So filming can often be a bit tricky – lots of unanswered questions like, 'Where did the Greyhound come from?', and 'Why did Angela suddenly attract a stalker?' But actually, it's not all that uncommon in television drama to film a later episode first as it gives the cast and crew a little bit of leeway to turn themselves into a 'lean, mean filming machine'.

The publicity for a big series seems to be centred around that all-important

ABOVE: Tom Craig, Jonathan Guy Lewis and Ian Curtis who play Fusilier Jacko Barton, Sergeant Chris McCleod and Corporal Mark Hobbs. McCleod demands to know where Barton and Hobbs have put his doughnut.

launch and first episode. People always want a pigeon-hole to put things in – so they know where they are. 'If it's a good first episode, ah well, then it's going to be a good series', 'Vintage "Soldier, Soldier"', etc, etc.

Eleven o'clock. Sticky bun o'clock. I'd forgotten what joy there was to be had in a world with sticky buns in it. The guy from Set Meals arrives like the Queen of Sheba. Wicker basket aloft. I can hear Handel, Purcell, trumpets. Can I really have the strength to limit myself to just the one? Surely one seems so cruel and lonely. Won't it take at least two – they're only small after all – to raise my blood sugar level out of the danger zone? And a banana as well, because I've seen the tennis players on telly eat them for energy; and an apple, because that cancels out the second sticky bun. You see, these are the crucial decisions that are constantly being made on set. This is what takes the time. Forget learning lines, or worrying about the character and story lines. It's whether to have that hash brown with or without the black pudding as well as the bacon and eggs – eggs got to be poached – this is cholesterol we're talking about; sticky bun time, lunch time, tea time, and 'this is ridiculous, we should have been wrapped hours ago' time. (Wrapped, of course, meaning allowed to go home.)

Last year, I only threw the one wobbler – totally out of character – but I think the pressure had been getting to me, and that was to do with tea. For days and days, every time they brought the tea out to the set (proper tea at four o'clock with sandwiches and cake and snacky bits), I'd missed out because I was involved in the action that was being filmed right at that moment.

Unlike all the other meals on set, where you have a break to have them, tea time at four o'clock is a cross between a lottery and a bun fight And I was pretty sick that I'd missed out so often. So, one afternoon, I just turned into Harry Enfield's adolescent character, Kevin, and very publicly threw lots of empty trays in the air – covering myself in lots of little bits of cress from the egg sandwiches and I remember bits of ginger cake going down my collar. The irony was that it proved hugely successful. After that, there was always a tray especially labelled 'Jonathan's tea'. Or it could have been, 'That w****r over there's tea'. I never could quite make out the lettering. It could just have been a very unusual way of spelling Jonathan.

Again I find myself in the deep end as my first scene this year is where Chris confronts Angela's stalker, who works on a fruit and veg stall in an Aldershot market, beating the crap out of him. No cosy little two-shot this! There's a stunt arranger, crowd and stall owners, as well as the good folk of Wokingham as an ever-present audience. I introduce myself to Scot Williams (ideal casting: Timothy Hutton – the son in 'Ordinary People') who is playing Neville Rigby, the stalker. It never ceases to amaze me how bizarre this whole business is. One minute it's 'Hello Scot, I'm Jonathan' (ideal casting: Brad Pitt; no, Ken Branagh, as neither of us have a top lip). The next minute, I'm throwing a right hook to his jaw followed by a nasty old knee in the privates, much to the pleasure of the ever-growing Wokingham locals. 'That's right, Chris [my character is Chris McCleod], you give him one!' Jason White, the stunt and fight co-ordinator (ideal casting: Ed Harris – 'The Right Stuff') gets Scot and me in a room for a few minutes. He gets us to stretch and warm-up before we rehearse and perfect the fight. There's nothing more naff than a fight that's supposed to look nasty and isn't, and Scot and I are anxious to put the time in to make it look real.

Above: Chris McCleod spots Rigby the stalker in the market...and is then hauled away in front of an appreciative audience to become a regular in 'The Bill'.
Right: Here's me doing my Prince Charles acting: 'one's acting always comes from one's gloves.'

Unfortunately, when filming, there never is enough of that most precious of commodities – time. Time is, as they say, 'Money'! We get the 'Turn over, background action, ACTION!' I hit Scot. He goes down, I pick him up and throw him against the stall and do the hit to his face. However, Scot doesn't get up from the stall. He is hunched over the swede. 'Stop. Stop. Stop.' 'What? But I didn't touch him governor, honest. It was close. But not that close.' Scot has just ricked his neck. 'Maybe it's the effects of that car crash I had two weeks ago', he suddenly announces. And I tell Jason I'd feel much happier throwing the punch with my left hand as I'm left-handed. 'Now they tell us', Jason says.

Thursday 6 February Episode 3

5.30am pick-up. Quite reasonable compared to yesterday. It gives me at least an extra twenty minutes sleep. I stumbled out of bed, or was I pushed? Miranda, my wife, grunts something into her pillow (ideal casting: Michelle Pfeiffer. I have to say that or I'll be sleeping in the garden shed). The one word I make out is Abraham (ideal casting: Abraham) so I guess she's saying something to do with not waking him up. I stagger to the bathroom. One of my indulgences from last year's series is the acquisition of a power shower. As I learnt last year, forget trying to have a bath at five in the morning. A couple of times I was so tired, I fell asleep in it, only to have the door bell rung by an anxious driver, worried that I had overslept. But this was nothing compared to the wrath of an irate wife left behind holding a woken-up baby.

My bag and all my clothes are laid out in the living room and it really does still feel like the middle of the night as I creep up the stairs and close the front door and hop into the Previa which has been waiting for me. (A Previa, by the way, is the large 'people moving' vehicle – very large, very comfortable. They are used to take us actors on location. It always feels like I'm being taken to school when I get in one – a very posh boarding school.)

BEHIND-THE-SCENES:

Life in the office

While we film one episode, there is frantic activity in the office as they finalise the script for the next one, recce all the various locations required, build and dress sets, hire actors who are coming in for just the one episode, and getting the filming schedule sorted out. This can be a nightmare in itself as some locations may only be available on certain days, or certain times, and sometimes they clash. You name it, they'll have to deal with it.

My driver this morning is Howard again. You know, the one whose ideal casting is Danny DeVito. Now, Howard looks about 12 years old, and a mischievous 12-year-old at that. He's very small and rather eccentric and always looks like he's been summoned to see the headmaster after being caught trying to blow up the chemistry labs. Unfortunately, Howard is particularly talkative for 5.30 in the morning, and eventually I have to make it horribly clear to him that an extra hour of sleep is rather more important to me than the pros and cons of the extra large lithium battery and exchanging messages on the voice mail of our mobile phones.

The journey time from my flat in north London to the location this morning is about ninety minutes. Or, as Howard would prefer to say, 'Our ETA this morning is approximately 7am.' However, if we were making the journey any time after 7am, commuter and rush-hour traffic would more than double that journey time. Not for Howard, though, no sir. Out pops his Route Master. 'Go on. Any location. Punch it in. This will give you a route which is constantly being updated to avoid any hold up, big or small.'

'Wake up, we're here', were more often than not the first words spoken to me on arrival at any location. But this morning, when we arrived at Sandhurst, I felt a huge surge in the pit of my stomach. It's more than 15 years since I was last here, but that intervening time seemed to evaporate in an instant as I looked up at Victory College.

I was sponsored by the army through my sixth form years at St Dunstan's College, an independent school for boys in south-east London, after winning a prestigious Army scholarship at the age of fifteen. I was then given a bursary by the army which helped to support me through my degree course in politics and society at Exeter University. I always remember when I first arrived at Exeter all those students sponsored by the army receiving a lecture from a Colonel dispatched from the Ministry of Defence to warn those naive, fresh faced, teenage, boy/men, of the perils of mixing with 'CND supporters, hunt saboteurs, homosexuals and, undoubtedly the most dangerous of all, sociology students.' I tentatively put up my hand and told the crusty old gentleman that, 'Well, actually, I too am doing sociology.'

A sea of faces swivelled round to scrutinise the infiltrator. 'Oh,' said the colonel. That was all he could say. 'Oh.' It was obviously the first time he'd seen one up that close; in the wild, so to speak. He took a very protracted and public mental photograph of me for the back room boys at the MOD. Just in case. In case of what, I don't know.

I'm sure we all have a physical memory of things that our bodies have been through, and my legs immediately turned to jelly when I saw the scaffolding towers on the edge of the assault course. They always had you up there leaping around after you'd done the most gruelling part of the course, just when your legs felt like jelly. It's nice this time to be playing the sergeant who tells them what to do, as opposed to being the one up there on the receiving end.

Today is also my first day working with Tom. Tom Craig is playing Fusilier Barton in this year's series. 'Jacko' to his mates. (Ideal casting: Steven Waddington, from 'Carrington' and 'The Last of the Mohicans' – no, he wouldn't like that, Tom's too much of a contemporary. What about the ginger actor from 'NYPD Blue', David Caruso? No, having just spoken to Tom, he says his ideal casting of himself would be James Cagney. Apparently, James Cagney had red hair. 'But he got away with it because it was all in black and white then.') Tom actually played a soldier, a Gunner, in the first play I wrote, 'Our Boys', which I directed back in 1993, and we've remained close friends ever since. His character in my play was a squaddie called Mick Speedy.

So playing a soldier is nothing new for Tom, who trained and worked as a plumber for six years before deciding to chuck it all in and come down to London and go to drama school. And that's one thing I love about Tom. Because he's had another life outside of acting, he's not afraid of saying exactly what he thinks.

Sometimes, as we all know, we can get a bit precious in this business. Maybe some of you reading this diary might think that of what I'm writing. But Tom knows what it's like to do a hard physical job and it's always refreshing working with him because he has a passion for acting, but it's always tempered with proportion. I know from many of the letters I've received that we do provide an important service, whether it be entertainment or escapism. But at the end of the day, we're not saving people's lives in a hospital. We put on costumes and pretend. And I think it's always healthy to remember that.

Wednesday 12 February Episode 3

Not been in since last Thursday – nearly a week. It always feels weird when it gets bitty like this. On some episodes, usually the more domestic orientated, all my scenes can be crammed into a couple of days, unlike the episodes with more of the military stuff. That tends to involve more of us more of the time, maybe even five or six out of the allotted filming days per episode (between 11 and 17 days).

Today, I had to do a scene in Reading town centre. I've raced over to the recruiting office where Angela – played by Fiona Bell (ideal casting: Sean Young or Emma Thompson, because you've got to have Emma T. in there somewhere, or it won't get made) – now works. Chris has realised she's there and that she is being confronted by her masked attacker – dramatic stuff! Chris pulls up, jumps out just as she gets away from him, and she rushes into his arms.

That was the theory, or the fantasy, depending on how you look at it. But when it came to it, I pulled up in my 'gun metal grey' BMW – automatic – 3 series (Chris is obviously doing quite well without Angela, thank you very much), jump out and run over to Fiona, who has just emerged from the building. But I then suddenly notice that no one seems at all interested in me or Fiona. Everyone is looking right past us and starting to cry out in panicked gibberish. Fiona and I turn round to see my 'BMDub', as the drivers from 'Action Cars' lovingly call it, careering towards a large, grey, and imposing statue of Queen Victoria. I can just make out a pair of feet sticking out horizontally from

LEFT: Tom Craig plays Fusilier Jacko Barton.

BELOW: Fiona Bell is Sergeant Angela McCleod, wife of Chris McCleod.

THE TECHNICALITIES:

The first, second and third ADs

The first AD is really the top dog on 'the floor', ie the film set. (Don't tell the director that.) Everyone involved in the actual day-to-day running of the filming is answerable to the first. We've had a number of firsts on the show, as they alternate between episodes, organising and preparing the episode before shooting it, while the other is doing the same for the next episode – visiting potential locations, drawing up the day-by-day shooting schedule with the second AD (which is another job altogether).
Edward Brett (ideal casting: Keanu Reeves with grey hair), who has 'firsted' on many of the major classy dramas, including 'Morse', 'Kavanagh QC', 'Poirot', and series Three, Four and Five of Soldier, and has the reputation in the business of being the consummate first AD, told me that the primary consideration of the first is to make possible, wherever possible, whatever the director wants.

Of course, every film set is run slightly differently, depending on the personalities and chemistry of the team gathered together. All the ADs have these rather FBI-looking ear pieces and have this tendency to glaze over when you start talking to them. Then suddenly they grip a cable on the lapel and talk furtively to their jackets – very disconcerting – especially when Edward and Adam Goodman, who often works as Edward's second AD, do look like possible FBI agents – tall, wholesome boys from Tennessee.

The second AD controls everything from the unit base. The only way to describe the mass of cars, caravans and coaches, Portacabins, Portaloos, vehicles, and generators, cables, and grubby looking tinkers – which is what the unit base always looks like – is to say, imagine being at a fairground without all the rides. All the fumes but none of the sparkle.

There are lots of unit and facilities drivers, who are always the first people to go to if you need to find out anything important like, have Carlton commissioned another series of 'Soldier, Soldier'? When's it going to be starting? And am I in it?

Martin, the third AD on 'Soldier, Soldier', has a particularly difficult job on the set. He has to put up with everyone blaming him for anything going wrong. Whether it be a group of extras not moving at the right time through the background of a scene, or if I suddenly 'dry' and can't remember for the life of me what on earth I say next, I just turn round and say, 'Oh I'm sorry everybody, that was Martin's fault!' That is a slight exaggeration, of course. I might only say, 'Oh Christ, Martin!' No, really, it is a very tricky job. As the Third, you're responsible for keeping the actors happy.

Martin, the third AD, 'I thought they said this was a professional outfit'.

Martin is also responsible for organising the background action in any scene. This means that all those people or cars that come in and out of a scene so nonchalantly have been planned, directed, rehearsed, just like a professional tennis player who makes the game look so easy. If the background action wasn't there you'd miss it, but if there was too much of it your attention would be drawn to that rather than the main action of the scene.

Luckily for Martin, he has the assistance of another third/runner, Jane (ideal casting: Kate Winslett, 'Sense and Sensibility', or Carol Vordeman, 'Countdown') who is more directly responsible for shepherding the actors to wherever they're supposed to be at any particular time, whether it be getting them into make-up first thing in the morning, or getting cups of tea. I'm afraid you do start to get into bad habits very quickly. At the beginning of the shooting, it's, 'No, Jane. Don't worry. I'll get it. No. Really. You stay there.' But after a few weeks, no, a few days, it's, 'Jane! Where's that tea? I said tea, love. Two sugars, and I want it now. So please drop that very expensive prop and get it for me now darling!' And, of course, everyone becomes 'love' and 'darling'. Purely because no one can remember anyone's name.

the driver's seat. They are Martin's feet. Martin (ideal casting: Patrick Swayze) is the 'third'. When I say Martin is the 'third', that's not like Richard the Third, or Edward the Second, what it means is Martin is the third AD or assistant director. He'd just managed to stop the car from destroying a major artefact of Reading town centre. 'Who needs a hand brake anyway?' he says, looking over at me, and I have to admit very sheepishly that I must have left it off. 'Oh I see,' he says, 'you were acting!'

Struggled with two Danishes, a doughnut and a Cadbury's mini roll – lost!

Picked a fight with a driver over the tea table. That was my mini roll. It had my name on.

And: 'Adam, I've been wondering, why are the loos always referred to as the "honey wagon"?'

Answer: 'Do you know, Jonathan, I haven't got a clue.'

Friday 14 February Episode 3

Valentine's Day. Well, sadly, Cindy Crawford's Valentine card never arrived. Perhaps she sent it to the wrong address. We have only just moved in after all.

Maybe that's what happened to all the other Valentine's cards that I didn't receive. And I was convinced there'd be a whole pile waiting for me at work. What about all the girls in make-up – Karen (ideal casting: Meryl Streep in a brown wig), Ali (Shirley MacLaine) and Ashley (Elle Macpherson)? The girls in wardrobe – Rachel (Sally Field), Tracey (Gina Lollobrigida)? Jane the floor runner? All the girls in the office and Helen Flint, the production manager? What about Annie Tricklebank (Deborah Winger), the producer? No, not a peep. Not a 'sossage'. I don't understand. It was the same last year. What's wrong with them? Why does one always expect a mail sack full, well, all right then maybe more realistically one or two? When at the end of the day, you're lucky if your other half, if you've got another half, only just remembers. Actually, M is always very good. Very funny. Sends cards and idiosyncratic presents that I really wish I had found and sent first.

Today, I went off to meet Sian Facer (ideal casting: Holly Hunter) who works in the licensing department at Carlton to tell her of my stunningly original idea for a diary of the series. A record in pictures and words of the series, alongside interviews with the other actors, and an attempt to explain what really does go on behind the scenes of a large and hugely popular TV drama. What everyone does, etc. What exactly is the gaffer? Or the best boy? What does the grip do? I wasn't sure of many of these technical things myself – so I thought it would be a good excuse to find out, without looking like an idiot, as I had the excuse of the diary to hide my ignorance. And I also wanted something to silence all those people who, on meeting you, think

BELOW: 'Not all the stars are in front of the camera,' says Keith from wardrobe. Here also are Ali from make-up and Tracey from wardrobe.

they're being incredibly witty when they find out you're an actor on 'Soldier, Soldier' by immediately enquiring whether you are going to be releasing a single. Thank you for that legacy Mr Green and Mr Flynn. And no I don't know them personally, as I joined the series just after they had left.

Anyway, I'd mentioned the idea of the diary to Annie (she of producer fame) a few weeks earlier, and she'd put me on to Sian. We'd spoken on the phone to arrange the meeting and I was terribly nervous when I arrived at the Carlton offices in Portman Square, just off Oxford Street. I always get a bit vague and blustery when I try to put on my confident disguise. I suppose what it is, is that I think that I'm putting on a cloak of swaggering intelligence and supreme, 'I know what I'm doing so you can trust me' confidence, whereas what really comes across is a public school air of arrogance mixed with, 'I don't think he knows what he's talking about' syndrome. It doesn't help, of course, when you get so nervous that you start a sentence and then half way through forget what it is you were going to say, and stare ahead blankly, desperately trying to look like another incredibly interesting idea has just entered your head, but you don't quite know how to express it!

I have to admit my so-called coolness was blown on arrival when I told the mega-efficient receptionist with shoulder pads from Dallas that I had an appointment with a Sian Facit. She looked at me blankly:

ABOVE: Tom Craig and Michelle Butterly:Photo Love or 'Soldier, Soldier'?
RIGHT: Chris Gascoyne plays Fusilier Tony Rossi – one mean machine riding another.

DUCATI
Agip

RECEPTIONIST Sian Facit. We don't have a Sian Facit.

ME (pulling out a grubby piece of kitchen roll which had the name written on it as well as some of Abraham's breakfast bran flakes to show her) But that's who I'm meeting. Sian Facit. There it is. (In black and white. And purple, and 3D browny bits.)

I could see a flash of 'he must either be a nutter or an eccentric writer who knows the chairman'.

RECEPTIONIST (grudgingly) We have a Sian Facer.

Perhaps she knew all along and had been winding me up.

When I met Sian she was very warm and receptive to the idea and said she would put together a package to send to all those publishing houses that do TV tie-ins (as this sort of book is called). Tense and tricky situation though during meeting as Sian could only offer Digestives with tea. But tea was Earl Grey, so Digestives acceptable – just!

Saturday 15 February Episode 3

6.15am pick-up. We then wait for Chris Gascoyne who plays Tony Rossi (ideal casting: Al Pacino – see previous page). I think he's got the wrong idea with his 6.45 pick-up time. He seems to see it as his wake-up time, and when he finally does emerge 15 minutes later, he still has sheet imprints on the side of his head. He can't conjure with language until he has finished his first cigarette – now feeling tinges of jealousy because it's just dawned on me he's had half an hour more sleep than me.

More of the assault course scenes at Sandhurst to finish. This was followed by some drive-by scenes in Wokingham of me on the way to Angela, the masked stalker and the statue of Queen Victoria (see box, opposite).

There were two bits of driving in this set-up that they needed to get, but they were always 'chasing the light', as they say. This tends to happen at the end of the filming day. It becomes a mad scramble to get as much done as possible of what was scheduled for that day before it gets too dark to film. Realistically roughly five minutes of usable footage per day needs to be shot, as a drama on ITV will have about five minutes of commercial breaks. When you see the dramas imported from America, it's possible to see quite clearly where the breaks should have been. And it's normally twice as many as we have to have in this country. Needless to say, we didn't quite get the second of the two shots. The first was just driving through the Saturday afternoon traffic of Wokingham High Street.

The second was filming my point-of-view (POV) of having to pull away at speed from some traffic lights. The problem came because none of the other Wokingham drivers had been told that that's what we were trying to do. And they didn't take too kindly to this 'git' driving the 'BMDub' trying to push in at the head of the queue. However, it wasn't actually that vital to get all of these shots as they were only going to be used as 'cut aways' from the main action (Angela being frightened by Rigby, her stalker), to build up the drama and tension.

I had enough tension as I was trying to watch 'Final Score' through the front window of a cottage on Wokingham High Street, while they rigged up my 'BMDub'. No sound. But Spurs lose again. Felt desolate. Watch Five Nations

THE TECHNICALITIES:

Filming a drive-by

Today, the first drive-by was filmed by a camera rigged up on a frame on the bonnet of the 'BMDub'. All the essential members of the crew – director Paul Brown, hunched over a monitor, Havana cigar in hand (ideal casting: Cecil B. de Mille), which shows him what the camera sees, while the first AD, director of photography, camera operator and focus puller, are crammed onto the low-loader which travels just in front of the car. Sometimes the car is attached to the low-loader, as in this case, which means when it looks like I'm driving, I'm really doing a tap dance. Last year, Fiona, who plays my wife Angela, had to do a few driving scenes and she would often get herself into a bit of a panic as she doesn't actually drive, or she didn't then. However, if you saw those scenes, of us driving along, you would have thought she was a veteran of the Paris to Dacca rally. It's amazing how much can be hidden by the technical tricks of the trade.

The same thing happened last year when the girls had to leap out of a plane doing a charity parachute jump in episode twelve. When you see the scene of them jumping out, you would have sworn they were jumping out of a real plane, thousands of feet in the air. In reality, we were in the back of the plane on the hot tarmac, with the wind machine going like the clappers, jumping onto huge plastic cushioned mats, surrounded by a very sweaty and pissed-off crew.

The second drive-by scene involved putting the camera in the back of the car. I always find these set-ups rather hysterical. They remind me of the Pink Panther film, where Peter Sellers is disguised as a gangster and crammed into the lift with several of the bad guys, and he does a fart. There I am, luxuriating in the acres of space in the driver's seat, and out of the corner of my eye I can see the director, the camera operator plus camera, focus puller, a couple of lights and a microphone on a fixed arm, and I've got the clapper board on my lap. It looks like the joke, 'how many elephants can you get into a mini?' The clapper board, by the way, is to identify the shot. When the whole thing is edited, the editor then knows which bit is which. The clap part of it is also a sound record which does the same thing, matching the sound to when we open our mouths.

snippets. Try not to sneak a look at score as intend to watch highlights on 'Rugby Special'. Obviously look like a vagabond as I'm whisked away to sit in Shaun (ideal casting: Baloo from 'The Jungle Book', or any large German tourist) Matthew's Jag (Shaun is the quartermaster and unit driver who drives the director, and anyone generally important enough to warrant a trip in his sparkling white Jag). Someone worried I might cause a fight. I think they confuse desolation for self-mutilation. Shaun tells me the scores. Potential enjoyment for rest of weekend gone. More desolation and steamy windows although this is tempered with curiosity at why I'm being allowed to wait in a VIP car. Then realise it is the only car. All the others have disappeared.

Shaun's such good value to have around. Last year he was one of the Previa drivers. This year, however, Shaun has worked his way up the driving ladder. He's bought himself a 'tasty motor' to drive the important people. He also does close protection and bodyguarding work, so is a very useful person to have around the place – preventing the stampeding hordes of fans who continually make my life a living hell! Well, there was one old drunk who shouted 'Oi! "Soldier, Soldier"' in my direction in Reading town centre the other day. But then we realised he was only a mate of mine.

I miss Shaun driving us home. We still try to keep up the old chats every once in a while. He's an all-round Mr Fixit and is worth his weight in gold. He's so committed to the show and works such long hours.

Things can only get better

Tuesday 18 February Episode 2

This is the first day of filming on episode 2, with Graham Moore directing. Graham directed a couple of episodes last year, so I know what to expect! Gascoyne still confused about pick-up time not being wake-up time. Still, at least he's consistent – 15 minutes between arrival outside his place and appearance of actor.

We spend from midday until six doing two parade ground scenes. How the hell some of the later stuff is going to match the footage shot earlier in the day I do not know. The light was completely different – winter darkness shrouding the parade ground in an inhospitable veil of translucence. Hello – I'm sorry. I suddenly slipped into Edgar Allan Poe. This really did feel like the bleak midwinter. Good luck Chris Howard, the series' director of photography (DOP). It is amazing how a talented DOP can conjure dusk out of practically any time of day in this country. Things get more difficult the nearer one is to the equator – in Africa, for example, the sun is directly overhead and throws shadows everywhere for much of the day.

Today, however, it is cold, cold, cold and it's my first time at Bearwood College. Most of the parade ground exteriors and some interiors are to be shot here over the course of the next six months. It's a school – partly boarding and with a distinctly naval association. There's a lifesize dummy in the entrance hall to this huge Gothic entity, completely kitted out in the old merchant navy uniform. He looks a dead ringer for 'Albert RN', the dummy from the old war-time prisoner-of-war film. The house looks like it's straight out of 'The Hound of the Baskervilles'. And I feel terribly sorry for all the boys and girls who have to be here.

RIGHT: Conor Mullen the tough new Company Sergeant Major – after finding out he's sharing a caravan with me.

The first of the two scenes is the arrival of Company Sgt Major Alan Fitzpatrick, played by Conor Mullen. It's a great entrance. The classic one with the arrival of a Land Rover; cut away to a pair of shining boots getting out, and the Land Rover pulling away to reveal the dear old CSM. On the first take I bark out the order to the assembled company, 'Stand still and wait for the new CSM', and we watch as the Land Rover drives up. It stops and we hear the door open, then close. But there's no pull away. The Land Rover has stalled.

It's my first scene with Conor (ideal casting: Steve McQueen from 'Bullitt'). I know I'm going to really like Conor. How is it you just know that about some people? He has a wonderful glint in the eye – very charming. Tells us about 'Reckless', which he filmed for Granada with Robson Green and the beautiful Francesca Annis.

In the second scene, Fitzpatrick tells Chris McCleod to get a greyhound from out of the driving cab of a four-tonner. The boys have supposedly hidden it there to get it out of the way. With bright ideas like that, of course that is why they will always be squaddies. I have to say that the old adage, 'never work with children or animals', is so true. Last year I had to contend with the lovely Leigh who played my son, Liam, stealing every scene we were in together. His beautiful, cherubic, blonde curls and radiant blue eyes melting every ones' hearts. This year it's a bloody dog!

After Chris McCleod had retrieved her from the four-tonner she was supposed to walk along the front line of Fusiliers and pick out Butcher, played by Danny Cunningham (ideal casting: the young cute one from Baywatch), as her master. But, of course, every time I let her go she went straight to her real owner who was obviously very fond of the ex-racer. The greyhound was quivering with fright and the greyhound's trainer proceeded to tell Conor and me

THE TECHNICALITIES:

The second unit

This is a second, smaller crew which operates simultaneously with the main unit. And it may only be for a few days to finish off all those little bits that never quite got done when they were originally scheduled. The second unit is also responsible for what are called 'pick-up shots', which are shots that the director or the editor need once they've started editing it, such as for linking segments to get from one scene to another. It's obviously very expensive having two units out at the same time, so quite often scenes are dropped to make sure that less needs to be filmed on a second unit.

LEFT: Graham Moore (director of episode 2), Lucy Cohu and me. Graham is telling us not to try to escape again.

that the reason the dog was shaking was because we had frightened her. Our shouting at the soldiers on parade had sent her into a tizzy. We chatted about greyhounds for a while. I felt so bad about the way the dog was looking at me. 'He shouts a lot. I don't like him', is what seemed to be in the dog's eyes.

The trainer then tells me how sensitive and affectionate Greyhounds are. Great. Thanks a lot. That makes me feel much better. She then went on to tell me how thousands of them are destroyed every year when they've been discarded at the end of their racing careers. But apparently they do make very good house pets, she added. For quiet families, obviously! We never did quite finish the scene, so the remaining shots will probably have to be carried over to what's called second unit (see box, opposite).

Saturday 22 February
Episode 2

Pick-up at 3.15pm. What a nice way to spend your Saturday night! It's actually a remarkably warm evening for February – very still, no wind. We're doing the briefing scene in the woods. And it's actually the same place as where we filmed the blowing up of the café on the lake in episode 6 last year. It's so still and quiet you would think you were on a massive sound stage for a multi-million dollar movie.

It's the first time I've seen Ben Nealon this year (ideal casting: Jim Carrey) who plays the part of Captain Jeremy Forsythe. Our paths have not crossed during the filming until now.

Above: Ben Nealon (Captain Jeremy Forsythe) auditioning for a musical over the phone.

I find out that on yesterday's night shoot Chris Gascoyne broke a bone in his hand, when he slipped and fell down an embankment. He should have gone straight off to casualty to get it seen to, but he was so cold he said it numbed the pain, and he carried on until four or five in the morning like a real trooper and saved the day or rather the night shoot by being so brave. This reminds me of last year when Dave Groves (ideal casting: Tony Curtis), who played Joe Farrell, broke his leg. And the ironic thing with Dave was that he didn't even do it at work. He did it one Sunday while he was moving house.

I meet Lucy Cohu for the first time as well. Lucy (ideal casting: Sigourney Weaver) is playing Major Bailey and we chat about Africa and how excited we all are about going.

Suddenly, a rain machine has been turned on. I forgot this scene is supposed to be set in the pouring rain. Always looks very odd – you wet, everyone else bone dry. Oh, I do love this job. It certainly beats working for a living. It's so silly and we all take it so seriously.

Monday 24 February Episode 2

Up most of the night with Abraham. He woke at 1am being sick, and was obviously very frightened as he didn't understand what was happening to him. He continued to vomit all over me as I took him to the bathroom. Isn't it funny, anyone else's vomit and it's a big no no, but when it's your child's, it's OK? Well, it's not exactly OK, but it is bearable. Up again at three and then at five – more vomiting, but by now there's nothing else to bring up and the retching is definitely causing him pain.

M and I take it in turns for the rest of the night. Reassuring the little mite by just being there is as much as you can do I suppose. And the trick in this situation is getting your shifts sorted out. One sleeps while the other rocks. Ah! Memories of the early days. Just after the breast feeding stopped and you no longer had the excuse to carry on sleeping while she fed him quietly.

ME It's your turn.
MIRANDA No, it's yours, I went last time.
ME No, that was the time before. You slept through the last time.

It's a 6.30am pick-up so I really am feeling and looking like shit. I meet Ravi for the first time. Ravi (ideal casting: Omar Sharif from 'Lawrence of Arabia') is driving me in this morning. He knows immediately from the way I look that it's been an all-nighter. He just asks, 'Self-inflicted or baby?' I'm so tired it takes me at least a minute to work out what self-inflicted means.

It turns out Rav's mum co-produced 'Ghandi' with Attenborough. Rav's an interesting and intelligent man; he has a degree in something Biotic, and knows about Jung. Finally I have to ask him, why is he driving for a living when he could be teaching, writing or making loads of money in business? Rav is definitely one of those people you just know could read up about something and then go away and be brilliant at it within a few weeks.

'Because I want to. Right now, it suits me.' He's worked on some interesting and big films. 'Schindler's List' in Poland, 'Braveheart' in Ireland and 'Remains of the Day'. But they were long hours – 14 hours a day is the norm, before overtime, six days a week. Ravi tells me how it's like the circus coming to town when a huge film crew descends on a location. The average size crew on something like 'Soldier, Soldier' is ninety. On a movie it can be upwards of twice that. On 'Braveheart' it was apparently more than two hundred. At one point there were more than 120 facilities trucks alone in Fort William. The hotel owner where Ravi stayed in Ireland said that he would do as much business in the bar on one night with a film crew in as he would in a whole week at high season.

Had words with Gascoyne about the concept of numbers. Did he know that they correlated to certain positions on a clock face, which if studied carefully could potentially let him know the correct time?

BEHIND-THE-SCENES:

A little light relief

Discover that Conor – CSM Fitzpatrick – is the speaking clock of Ireland. I'm star struck and over-awed.
ME How long did it take to record that?
CONOR Argh! It was just a matter of a few hours.
ME How's that?
CONOR Well, in Ireland, when they ask the time, what they get is : Look it's going on for eight. You better hurry up or you's be late.
(Silence)
CONOR That was a joke Jonathan!
(Silence)
ME So when you ring up to find out the time, it's you hearing yourself speak?
CONOR Yeeeeeeeeees. (With an upward crescendo)

RIGHT: Danny, Tom and Chris together with Primrose the greyhound, the real star of the show.

Wednesday 26 February Episode 2

Pick-up at 10.15am. Can this really be true? I can't sleep from about 7am. I'm terrified the doorbell's going to ring any moment. But no – 10.15 it was. Today, it's just the one scene for me. I do feel very much like a part-timer this year – so far. I wonder if that will change soon. Still, it's nice to make the most of time at home with M and the little one. To have a good and regular wage for seven months with all this time off as well.

I've always been told to believe and expect that actors should live in a garret and starve for their art. Well, if you set aside the fact that this is far from being art, it's been a pretty damn good job, so far. My motto is, 'make the most of it now, because it might not be as good as this tomorrow'.

Tuesday 4 March Episode 2

6.45am pick-up.

Suggested that Chris McCleod learnt a foreign language some time ago. Might be some scope for humour there. 'Sorry, it's been done before in a previous series.' 'Yes, but there's more than one foreign language.' From my dim and distant sojourn with the armed forces I seem to recollect they were very keen on all that sort of thing. They even gave you extra pay for proficiency in particularly important ones like Russian or Arabic. 'OK, you can do Russian.'

Today's the day after all that, and I do get to say: 'Moojick zaconchinney oobloodock' (phonetic spelling obviously), which roughly translates to, 'the man's a complete bastard.' Now that's quite a useful little ditty to have up your sleeve when you get lost in Bracknell on a Saturday night after closing time.

Feeling that I'm sharing a discovery with Gascoyne. Our journey in together in the mornings from northwest London has bonded us. It's not just a journey in a physical sense – it's becoming a journey in an educational sense. The hunt for punctuality. Will he ever be out of his flat on time?

The north London Previa has a very different atmosphere to the south London mob. Bob 'Heart attack' Lilley is the main driver for the south London club, which includes Danny Cunningham, Tom Craig and Ian Curtis. Bob (ideal casting: Andy Capp) won the name 'Heart attack' while working on 'Braveheart' in Ireland – due to obvious reasons as he ended up in an Irish hospital for a week. If you look carefully on the credits of 'Braveheart' you can even see 'Heart attack' immortalised in celluloid. Then there's Rav, the second driver, and John Dawson, the third driver (ideal casting: one of the warriors in 'Braveheart'). He, too, worked on 'Braveheart'. I keep expecting him to show up at my place with his face painted blue and white. He swings both ways – in the driving sense – he's not proud, he'll pick-up in both north and south London.

Some second unit stuff as well today. A few scenes that they weren't able to get within the main unit schedule. In this particular scene that we're filming today, the dog is in the boys' dormitory with Tony Rossi, Jacko Barton and Andy Butcher. They've prepared some dog food for the greyhound – whose name is 'Babe' in the series – and Butch is preparing to have another go at a crucial fitness test he has to pass. Suddenly, Chris McCleod hears a dog bark, and goes into their room, which is where the noise seemed to come from. But in the meantime, they've seen him coming and hide the dog in one of their lockers. Chris then discovers the dog food on the table and makes Butcher eat it, because Jacko tells him it's a special stew that they've made to help Butch get through his fitness test.

Divided we fall

Tuesday 18 March Episode 1

6am pick-up. Gascoyne fluent in numbers up to seven. He's still confused with fractions though. Hasn't equated thirty with half. As in six-thirty or half-past six. Started him off on big and little hand stuff. Given him homework for tomorrow.

More parade ground antics. It's amazing how a couple of Land Rovers and four-tonners can be made to look like the whole Royal Corps of Transport. Very clever use of the background action.

Haven't seen the boys for a couple of weeks. Chris's hand seems much better now, and at least the plaster's off, so they'll be able to film two hands instead of one. This morning we're shooting the arrival of the new CO, Lt Col Philip Drysdale – played by James Cosmo (ideal casting: David Caruso from 'NYPD Blue'. Good Lord! That man gets everywhere. How about Kirk Douglas?). James is built like Charlton Heston – BIG! He's a lovely gentle man and a terrific actor and it's a real asset to the series to have someone of James's calibre and stature at the acting helm.

Fiona (quick re-cap: Fiona Bell, who plays Chris McCleod's wife Angela) thinks she might have blown it with Jimmy, though, when she met him in the make-up bus. Instead of concentrating on his roles in 'Braveheart', 'Roughnecks' and 'Ivanhoe', she couldn't stop talking about how good he was in 'Take the High Road' all those years ago, 'when "Take the High Road" used to be good.' Apparently he sat nodding silently, as Fiona not only dug the hole but buried herself in it. And covered it over with stones.

I just know that one of these shots they're doing this morning, with all of us running along to the parade ground, is going to be used in the opening credits somewhere. It's got that opening credits feel to it – very 'Officer and a Gentlemany' sort of stuff. And due to excessive physical activity – I lost count how many times we ran the hundred metres to and from the parade ground (at least three or four) – and the cold, my blood sugar level fell below the acceptable, EU recommended, safe point. In technical parlance, it fell 'below the four Hobnob line'. On this special occasion, I felt it was the least I could do for my body's sake to mix Danish and doughnut.

Paul (Cecil B. de Mille) Brown is directing again. He did my first big one last year: episode 2, which had a lot of action in it, when I was shot and taken hostage. I remember in those early days being very keen to do my own stunts.

'No way,' said Paul. 'Go on. Trust me. I know what I'm doing.' (Sure sign when an actor says that, he is talking out of his backside!) Anyway, I'm glad I didn't do my own stunts.

In this particular episode there was an explosion just as my captor and hijacker, also confusingly called Paul, and I ran out of the ramshackle old barn where I'd been held hostage. We'd done all the interior shots the previous day with it snowing outside. This final effect was the icing on the cake of the night shoot. It took hours to rig up and there were two cameras set-up on different angles to catch what was supposed to be a fairly contained, but inevitably, one-off bang. When it came to it, we were all watching from at least fifty metres away as the two stunt guys doubling for Paul and me burst out of the barn. We were then rocked on our feet as a huge thunderous noise – to call it a bang would be a massive understatement – blew the roof off the barn. It was an explosion the like of which I have never seen. Not that I've seen that many explosions, of course.

Bits of flaming debris landed on the two stunt guys – one had eyelashes singed, the other a small burn on the wrist. They always douse their exposed skin with a flame resistant jelly which absorbs most of the heat just before the camera turns over. So to discover they had both been hurt and also quite a bit shaken by the size and impact of the blast made me realise very quickly that they are paid to take those risks, and they are trained to take those risks, whereas I'm not.

If they'd wanted us to tap dance out of the barn I could have obliged with a couple of buffaloes instead. But now I'm quite happy to let other people make me look good while I sit back and watch their efforts. One very useful bonus, though, was the fact that Glenn Marks, who was the stunt co-ordinator last year and doubled for me in the barn explosion, did look remarkably similar to me on screen. So if anyone did ever ask, I could always say, 'Yes, of course I do my own stunts. What do you think I am? A wimp?'

Still hung-up about 'honey wagon' and reason for it being called this. Surely it would have been more appropriate to call it the 'fly conveyance'.

ABOVE: Tom Craig and Chris Gascoyne with their stunt doubles, Dean and Andreas. RIGHT: James Cosmo: 'Get my agent on the phone, this tent is too small, they promised me a Winnebago.'

Saturday 22 March Episode 1

6am pick-up. Haven't seen the boys since Tuesday.

Slightly perturbed today as I found out my nickname is Chris McLOUD. All I seem to do in every scene I'm in is shout 'Go. Go. Go.' Starting to think I should have called this diary 'Go. Go. Go.'

More of Sandhurst today. Outside again. So feel justified to eat two doughnuts at elevenses. Afterwards, felt ashamed. Dirty. Fat. Andy from wardrobe tells me my trousers are looking a little tight round the middle. I tell him it's his imagination. Starting to get used to being at Sandhurst again. I've stopped

looking behind me, waiting for an instructor to bawl in my ear. Maybe that's subconsciously why I'm doing all the shouting. To get my own back. Hadn't thought of that.

Didn't finish the scene. Again. The boys laid a good 30 metres of track (see box, below) and then had to take it up again.

Monday 24 March Episode 1

Salisbury Plain for a week. No commuting – staying in the Bishopstrow House hotel. Possibly the most luxurious place I've ever stayed in. It's a big old Georgian mansion with indoor swimming pool, indoor tennis, a great dining room – heaven. We stayed here last year right at the beginning of filming. M was stuck at home with the little one having quite a hard time of things, and there I was in the lap of luxury. I had escaped and I was about to enjoy a whole week of unbroken sleep at night.

When I spoke to M on the phone in the evenings last year I had tried to play it down as I hadn't wanted to rub it in, and I think she was almost feeling sorry for me by the end of the week. So I decided there and then to arrange a weekend away at the Bishopstrow House for the three of us as soon I could. When the time came, and we arrived at the hotel, Miranda was gob smacked. As soon as we were left alone in our suite, which I have to say was larger than our flat, she suddenly turned round and walloped me – 'You never told me it was like this!' She was livid for at least five minutes.

My room this time is even better than before. Sitting room downstairs, galleried bedroom with Elizabethan four-poster upstairs. The big question was,

THE TECHNICALITIES:

The dolly and grip

The dolly is the contraption that the camera sits on along with the camera operator and focus puller. It moves on a track that resembles a small-gauge rail track as it is put together in approximately two foot lengths. It is very time-consuming as it all has to be dead level so that the camera on the dolly can run along it smoothly, with no bumps. The dolly is then operated by a person called the grip, whether pushing it along a length of track between pre-arranged marks, or elevating it up and down. And believe you me, the dolly is incredibly heavy. You don't mess around where that is concerned. Heavy and expensive – roughly the price of a small family car. But you couldn't do seventy going up the M1 on the back of a dolly. Well, feasibly I suppose you could. There just wouldn't be much leg room.

ABOVE: The dolly will be stopping at all stations to Aldershot barracks.

Above: Robin Cope, the military adviser, conducting The King's Own a capella choir on tour to Salisbury Plain.

'Do I tell Miranda or not?' Maybe I'll wait a bit. She's going to have it tough enough as it is this week with me away, because on top of that, she starts rehearsing a play which opens at the Young Vic in London in six weeks time. So for her it means a week of getting Abraham up, dressed, breakfasted and dropped at the childminder, before going on to work. It really amazes me how any single mother can work. The stress must be so enormous. I decide on honesty being the best policy, and tell her straight away that we're back at The Bishopstrow, but that I am in agony with a sprained ankle, which is also true.

Work was slow today. We rehearsed the opening scene – a company attack – from 8am until gone 3pm. Lots of effects and bombs going off and bangs and extras. There are rumours that the pyrotechnics alone were costing fifty thousand. There was only ever going to be the one go at this so everything had to be just right or the whole day would have been wasted. Robin Cope (ideal casting: Robert Redford), who is the military adviser, leads the way, showing us what's what – how a company attack works, etc, etc. He's only given a few minutes to try to turn us into something that would, at a distance, pass for the real thing.

Tuesday 25 March Episode 1

Documentary film crew out with us all week. Filming up everyone's noses. I twisted my ankle yesterday, going over on the hard, uneven ground so went to see the medics today to get it strapped up. There's always a nurse or paramedic on hand when you're filming, which is great because you can stock up for your medicine cabinet at home.

'Everything all right?' 'Well, not really. I'm feeling a bit run down. Do you think I could have tubs of vitamin C and B12, a box of multi-vitamins and minerals, and some cod liver oil capsules? Oh yes, and you had better pop in a box of Berrocas for me, as well; plus a large pack of Lemsips.' 'Yes. Those nice new ones with menthol.' 'Anything else for you sir, like shares in Boots?' 'Well, now you come to mention it, there is the small matter of my sprained ankle.' Within seconds there was a camera in my face.

'Would you just like to tell us what happened?' 'Is it serious?' This last question just as I'm asking the medic for a tube of Anusol. 'Got piles as well have we?' 'No, but it's a great hang-over cure for the eyes.' He looked at me blankly. It was a tip from my screen wife Angela. I came into make-up one morning last year and saw Fiona rubbing the stuff on the bags under her eyes. I stared at her – horrified.

Me — Those are bags not piles, love!
Fiona — Same principle. Smoothes out the skin. Pulls it taut.
Me — Just as long as you remember not to put eye-liner on your bum!

ABOVE: Corporal Hobbs (Ian Curtis) warning Angela McCleod (Fiona Bell) that any highland dancing would be totally inappropriate until they'd all finished the assault course.

It was another long day today. More company attacks. Still, at least the sun's out and we can get a bit of a tan. Not in front of the make-up girls though. Ali comes running round after us dabbing on liberal amounts of total sun block as any kind of tan can ruin continuity. Have to say it is understandable – would look a bit odd if one minute you were pink, and the next you were bronze.

One of the extras – Graham, 'Just call me Titch' (ideal casting: Oliver Twist or Christopher Robin) – is playing my radio op this week. We chat about babies. He has a little boy who's a month older than Abraham, called Joshua. Sadly, Joshua's got chicken pox. This time last year I went down with chicken pox. I had never felt so ill in my life. They even had to write me out of an episode because I was too ill and too infectious to work. Thankfully, I had just had the last episode off so I hadn't been in contact with anyone from the film set, because if I had, the insurance doctor said he would have had to close down the entire set for at least two weeks otherwise they would no longer have been completely insured.

Graham tells me that secretly he'd like to give up his job as a car salesman and be an actor. I tell him not to be too hasty and remember that most actors are unemployed more than they are employed. But then who am I to tell Graham not to do it? It's his life. As they say, 'You only regret the things you didn't do'.

Feeling rather paternal towards Graham. A little bit worried by this. Decided to change ideal casting from Oliver Twist to the Artful Dodger – and this is after only a few days of Graham's jokes.

Wednesday 26 March Episode 1

More manoeuvres. Beginning to think I've joined the bloody army for real. Don't they know we're actors, love? Stuck out on exercise in the middle of nowhere. Missing the family very much. Looking forward to getting back tomorrow night.

The sparks (electricians) have arranged a last night karaoke party. One of the extras, Billy Budd (ideal casting: Robbie Coltrane), excels himself. Must say I've never really got the hang of karaoke. Standing up and proving to everyone that I've got the voice of Lee Marvin isn't my idea of entertainment. Still, I feel better because Ben scored '*nil points*'. He took to the stage with the consummate professionalism and confidence of 'Van the Man' Morrison, whiskey in one hand, stool in the other, and then proceeded to turn into Val Doonican.

Chris Gascoyne is starting to turn into Al Pacino. Lots of black, hang dog eyes, beaten-up leather jacket and a fag stuck to the side of his mouth. He tells me he always gets a bit 'Yorkshiry' when it gets to chatting up the women – which is quite strange really, considering he comes from near Nottingham. It transpires that he means that he goes all knotted and brittle. Lots of nodding and 'all right' to anyone in a skirt.

BELOW: Chris Gascoyne. 'He won't take that leather coat off for nobody.'

Thursday 27 March Episode 1

Last day here. Ankle still sore. Maybe I'll try rubbing the Anusol on it. Seems to work everywhere else.

The stunts and explosions all look brilliant, and the two stunt guys who double for Tom Craig and Chris Gascoyne are dead ringers. They do a spring-board dive from an explosion which looks fantastic. I've just heard a great story about Paul Brown, the director, who edited all the earlier series of 'Soldier, Soldier'. Apparently, on his arrival here at the beginning of the week, he saw the target vehicles that the artillery and tanks practise live firing on, and they were painted the standard orange colour. He decided he wanted them painted red.

So at two o'clock in the morning, and by the light of some car headlights, all the target vehicles were painted red. This was not as stupid as we had initially thought, because having just seen some stills of the action around the target vehicles with all the explosions, you realise that the red, in fact provides a much better background than the orange they had once been. For a start, if the vehicles had been the original orange colour, they would have been masked by the fireballs from the explosions.

We don't leave Salisbury until 7pm, which means I don't get home until 9pm. Ravi tells me more of his incredible life story. His mum is an ex-TV star. She was the naked woman whose silhouette we see dancing at the beginning of the Bond film, 'Thunderball'. He tells me of his ballooning company in India and the Lithuanian ex-go-go dancer who he's been trying to help. Sending her money for her education. I suggest the obvious, but he assures me it's totally above board. And I believe it of him. He is a true gent and a real philanthropist. He gets a lot of pleasure from helping others. He says it's good karma.

Tuesday 1 April Episode 1

6am pick-up. Ring Chris en route, but he's already up. He's starting to get the hang of this time thing.

Lots and lots and lots of waiting today. I lose several fights with doughnuts and Danish pastries, and my pee is turning brown. It suddenly dawns on me that it's undiluted tea. Decided against a recycling experiment. It's funny what boredom can do to a brain. We play football against a wall, and regress to being 12 years old again. Ian Curtis (ideal casting: Ian Hart, Lewis Collins or Montgomery Clift), who plays Corporal Mark Hobbs, suggests a game of 'Shit Head', but the mood of the acting camp this year is distinctly anti-'Shit Head', as opposed to last year when you couldn't tear the boys away from the cards.

The lovely Chris Howard, director of photography (ideal casting: Kermit the Frog or Dustin Hoffman), tells Paul Brown at lunch time that there was something wrong with the camera. Apparently, we'd been shooting all morning without film. The blood rushed out of Paul's face, and he stopped chewing. He looks at Chris like the Tories were going to get elected for a fifth term. Chris can't go through with it, and admits that it was a wind-up. It is April Fool's Day after all.

John Dawson, the driver, tells me another story about the saintly Mel Gibson, of 'Braveheart'. It is one of those driver's fantasy stories that drivers talk about with awe for years after. Apparently, Mel was driven around in a very expensive Range Rover, with a twin this and double that, by his very trusted and loyal driver, 'Fat Freddie'. When the shoot finally came to an end, after months and months and months, and Mel was going home to LA, and he'd said all his goodbyes and given his thank-you gifts, Fat Freddie was doing his last task and driving Mel to the airport. When they got to the airport, Mel got out and just said goodbye – obviously thanking Freddie, but nothing else. Then suddenly Freddie remembers to ask Mel what he should do with the car. 'Keep it. It's yours,' came the reply.

BEHIND THE SCENES:

'Braveheart'

Jimmy Cosmo tells a very funny story about Mel Gibson while working on 'Braveheart'. When any of the actors, no matter how big or small, famous or unknown, fluffed a line, Mel would come rushing up and stick a squidgy red nose on them. And they'd have to do the next take wearing the nose. Jimmy said he'd escaped this almost right until the end of filming, but one morning when he was 'atop the battlements' with the camera miles below at the bottom looking up, he made a real humdinger of a fluff. Jimmy thought, no, Mel's not going to bother coming up all this way to stick the nose on.

But, sure enough, there was a 'cut' from down below, and this figure in the distance came out from behind the camera and started climbing up the several ladders and along the length of the battlements. And 'splat', Mel whacked the nose on the not-so-weeny frame of Mr Cosmo. Apparently there were laughs all round.

Presumably, all this means there is a more or less complete copy of 'Braveheart' – the multi-million dollar movie – with a red nose popping up on screen the entire time. Perhaps it's in Mel's personal collection. A unique memento of the film.

Above: Ian Curtis who plays Corporal Mark Hobbs: ' Wing mirror, wing mirror on the car, who's the fairest fusilier by far?'

Apparently, Mel Gibson had sorted out all the paper work and planned the whole thing. Obviously, one wonders how much has been distorted over the telling, but it must be fairly accurate as John was up there at the time, and Jimmy Cosmo also verified the story for me. I suddenly had visions of me throwing the keys of my Rover 216 to John, and saying, 'Take it, it's yours.' And him turning round with a smile that turns to a grimace when he sees the car and saying to me, 'No, you're all right. You can keep it,' as he throws the keys back at me.

Top: Jacko and Rossi flee from the carnage on Salisbury Plain ...
Above: ... but not quite fast enough.
Left: The catapults send the stunt doubles flying through the air.

How was it for you?

Saturday 5 April Episode 6

Graham Moore directing again. All day outside. It's the 15K tab with Major Bailey (Lucy Cohu). We're all supposedly carrying a 60-pound sand bag in our Bergens (backpacks) – ridiculous! Some of the extras, all of whom are ex-military, from an agency called 20/20, say this is almost impossible. Even the ex-Paras say they've never done it.

First-up was the water tunnel. It's very, very cold this morning and there's a biting wind. Why is it everyone's got wetsuits under their uniforms and I haven't? 'Oh,' says Andy from wardrobe, 'it doesn't say in the script that you go in the water.' He tells me this as I'm standing up to my waist in a very manky, chalky, water obstacle. 'Where did you think I'd be standing then, Andy? On top of the rope slide?'

The atmosphere got a bit tense in the afternoon as I wasn't entirely happy with the way things were going. I'm not advocating being a bolshie actor, just one who cares about the work and one who is aware that time constraints often mean compromises that do more harm than good to the final result. It can be very hard knowing that sometimes, with just a bit more time and balls, it could be so much better. This can only really come about because of the confidence and knowledge you pick up being with a series for the whole length of it being filmed. The actors who come in for just one episode, sometimes for just one or two days, have a much harder job. The pressure is enormous to get it right.

It was all too much. 'I told you we could make her cry.'

You also have to get used to the fact that, on the whole, no one tells you what to do unless it is wrong. In the beginning of my, albeit, limited TV career, I remember being worried, because having come from a largely theatrical background where there is constant feedback, I was suddenly thrust into situations where I'd do the scene, and there would be nothing. No comeback. Nothing. And I'd constantly be saying to the director, trying to catch his or her eye, 'Was that all right? Was I OK? Wasn't too big was it? Did I do enough?' It took this paranoid, insecure actor a long time to realise that there are so many other elements to the process to consider besides massaging my ego. I think the problem, however, lies in not ever being able to get enough rehearsal time for actors to establish a dialogue or shorthand with a director first. Sometimes on Soldier, an actor may only meet the director for the first time when they show up to do their scene or scenes.

Not mentioned Ian Curtis much until now because I've hardly seen him. Ian plays Corporal Mark Hobbs. Always wanted to call Hobbs 'Hotpoint' as a nickname, but it never seemed to stick. 'Hotpoint' as in Russell and Hobbs who make kettles and things. No one ever seemed to find that funny, though, apart from me. I thought it was very MASH.

Monday 7 April Episode 6

Today we are filming a scene between Corporal Mark Hobbs and Chris McCleod at the beginning of the episode when Chris returns to camp. They chat at the gates and Hobbs is on duty. However, the scene as it stands is not quite right. I feel that it could be utilised to say quite a few interesting things about Chris and Mark, and what's been happening to them both.

I rang Annie a couple of days ago to express my concern. She agreed, and said she would give it some thought. How she has time to do this among the thousand-and-one other things that are constantly needing her attention, I don't know. That's one of the skills of the producer, I suppose. Today, she's rushing around set, and you can always tell when Annie's on-set because you just have to look out for khaki trousers, Timberland boots and sandy bomber jacket. Apparently, even after all those days, episode 1 is still a few minutes light. They need another couple of scenes, which Annie is working on, about Butcher and Rossi going to visit Barton in hospital. But Annie spares a few minutes with Ian and me.

BEHIND-THE-SCENES:

Keeping cool

During the ultra-cold filming in the water tunnel, one of the extras defied belief. Dressed as a physical training instructor, he took the whole thing a little bit too seriously by spending the entire morning standing, legs akimbo, hands on hips, on top of the mound above the water chute, wearing just a sleeveless singlet and lightweight green trousers.
AN EXTRA He's ex-Foreign Legion.
ME What? French Foreign Legion?
EXTRA Is there any other?

RIGHT: Another hard day at the office.

THE WATER TUNNEL

TOP: An officer and a gentlewoman. Major Jessica Bailey keeps on going, despite Sergeant McCleod's attempts to lure her into the bushes.
ABOVE: Out she comes from the water tunnel (kind of damp but an infinitely better person for the experience).
RIGHT: Getting over it with Angela – Fiona, Lucy, a water bottle and a wheel.

I've tentatively re-written the scene with Ian. We think it reads and will play much better. Annie agrees. Instead of just saying that Chris has been away, he says that he's been visiting his son, Liam, in Northern Ireland. It's the only reference in the whole series to that story line from last year. And Hobbs tells Chris that he hasn't seen Kate and his kids for months, the sub-text for him being the start of his crack-up which is then going to last right through to the end of the series.

I'm still not happy over the way the story line with Chris's son has been so completely ignored. I've tried to say that with an issue such as absentee fathers, you really have to be careful. What are you trying to say about Chris? Especially now that I'm a father myself. You don't just walk away from something like that and I know that my character wouldn't. And even if they did want Chris to walk away, then some reference should be made to the whole area of absentee fathers. But, instead, the story line has been completely dropped. That was that series, this is now.

It's a shame, because I think it was a strong story line which came out of a very interesting, and plausible situation. And it was a story line that I think most people seemed to be interested in. However, the emphasis this year seems to be on the cheeky chappy humour. There doesn't seem to be as much room for the more interesting, harder-edged stuff.

Tuesday 8 April Episodes 6 and 1

It all feels a bit of a blur since my last entry (only last Saturday). Last night was a second unit night shoot on episode 1 – 17 days later! Someone joked that it was going to take the Wizard of Oz to edit the thing together. So much film, so many different set-ups.

After 17 days, there's bound to be a lot of inconsistencies in continuity, as much of it has been shot out of order. I'm sure my hair's a lot longer at the moment and there's the small matter of the 34 doughnuts! My God! Thirty-four! I nearly wrote 24 because I'm so embarrassed. Thinking about cutting the doughnut revelations altogether and keeping personal gluttony private.

Normally we have our hair cut every ten days or so. And everyone has to shave every day, even the girls. Unless you're playing a baddy, that is. If you're a baddy, then you can grow stubble and smoke. The nightmare at the moment is that with the second unit stuff still going on it means two episodes that don't chronologically follow each other (episodes 1 and 6) are being shot at the same time. The episodes are supposed to be designed as self-contained pieces of drama that can be watched, understood and enjoyed whether you've followed the series or not, but there are story lines that do carry on over. This makes the script writing process for the entire series quite a palaver.

Bronagh Taggart (ideal casting: Pamela Anderson. Only joking Bro! How about Jane Austen?), the script editor, has to juggle more balls than the Harlem Globetrotters, and one wonders how comfortable Bronagh would be playing defensive guard on the old basketball court. It's a shame we never see any writers out on set. I would have thought it would be nice for them to put names to faces to characters.

I have worked with one of the writers – Len Collin (ideal casting: Bob Hoskins in Michael Keaton's body) – in his capacity as an actor, but it was quite a few years ago now. More than I care to remember. We both played smooth photocopier salesmen in a fly-on-the-wall documentary-style corporate video. There was no script. It was all improvised. We had a real scream breezing in to offices, and trying to sell real business people fictional photocopying machines. We wore concealed radio mics and were followed at a discreet distance by a camera crew. The people in the offices either thought we were from 'The Cook Report' or 'Beadle's About'. All, that is, apart from one office in Covent Garden where Len's gift of the gab almost sold a photocopier for real. But as all week we'd been working on the 'no, no, no' response, we hadn't the first idea what to do when a potential client said yes. We were quite gob smacked, so we panicked and left.

Tom, Chris, and I rehearse the scene with me bollocking them, as Paul Brown, the director, and Chris Howard, the DOP, talk through the technicalities: how many set-ups, where to put lights, the rain machine. Tom and Chris Gascoyne stand at attention, bruised and bloodied, and we have the brainwave that I should make them put their thumbs in their mouths as I'm bollocking them, which will put even more emphasis on how childish their behaviour is. It seemed such a humiliating and yet funny thing to make them do. The crew loved it. Lots of laughs all round. We even did the first take like that, but then Paul came over and said he didn't like it. And, of course, he's the director, so

BEHIND-THE-SCENES:

Script changes

Here is a conversation I had with the director, Paul Brown, during today's filming.

PAUL Great staircase. Let's use the staircase. Bring McCleod down the staircase.

ME Why?

PAUL Because it looks great.

ME But what have I been doing up there?

PAUL Just come down the staircase.

So, for the first time in my career, I get to do the big walk down. It's the scene where Rossi and Barton have been fighting in the rain, Major Bailey discovers them and Chris is sent to deal with it.

I walk down what feels like a hundred steps, although at least a quarter of them are missing or wobbly . It's a wrought-iron staircase straight out of 'A Streetcar Named Desire'. I keep jutting my jaw out and shouting 'Stella', but no one takes a blind bit of notice. Either my impression of Marlon Brando is so bad they don't understand who it is and what it is I'm saying, or they don't know Streetcar, which I find hard to imagine. There is, of course, a third possibility – they do know what it is I'm doing, but they're choosing to ignore me in the hope that I'll knock it on the head and shut.up. Fat chance of that.

'Stella! Stella! Blanche! Stella!'

Madeleine Buckingham on continuity (ideal casting: Una Stubbs, or maybe Olive Oil from 'Popeye') even comes up to me clutching her big black book, which contains the script and a thousand-and-one bits of important technical information which she has to keep track of (like which size lens was used in which shot), and a very furrowed brow.

MADELEINE You're not really going to say that, are you?

ME I might do.

MADELEINE But there isn't a Stella. It's Rossi and Barton.

ME Yes. But McCleod's decided from now on to call Barton, Blanche and Rossi, Stella.

MADELEINE But you can't do that. It hasn't been passed by Bronagh.

ME Well, you'd better get her on the phone.

She was dialling the number before I could bring myself to stop her. Any last minute changes to the script have to be passed by the script department or Annie T, the producer, and it does get frustrating when they turn round and block a suggestion.

obviously we had to do the scene within his vision of it. But it is sometimes very frustrating when you think you've come up with something original and you aren't allowed to pursue it.

Someone in production has decided that McCleod should wear a belt with his combat jacket. Apparently he needs smartening up. It's funny they should think of this now. I spent the whole of the last series and nearly half of this one not wearing one. The idea behind not wearing one came from the real Para Sergeant who I went to see and follow around as part of my original research for Chris McCleod's character.

Evidently, the Paras, whose combat smock is different to other regiments, have a convention of not wearing belts. I'm not sure quite why, but I think it may have something to do with parachutes and getting tangled up and that sort of thing. But now I'm told that every unit has its own 'Standing Orders', and within that its own idiosyncrasies concerning dress code, and that the King's Own insist on all the men wearing belts. Well, why didn't you say so in the first place?

This is my last shoot on episode 1. 'Soldier, Soldier – the movie' continues down at the dog track. Comparisons are made to the epic Chariot racing scene in 'Ben Hur', but sadly I'm not involved in the greyhound racing scenes, so I can but 'spectate on second-hand reports from the fray anon.'

Home by 3.30am. On sofa bed. I don't want to incur the wrath of woken Zombie woman. It could mean baby duties all day for me if I do.

TOP: Tom tries to serenade Ben in the back of the Land Rover, with a fist of help from Chris. ABOVE: Simon Okin with all his sound gear. 'Forget this for a game of soldiers. I'm turning back, the road's blocked off.'

LEFT: On the set with Jo Phillips-Lane (Karen Fitzpatrick). One of the three occasions we actually met on set.
BELOW LEFT: Conor Mullen with Michelle Butterly. 'Look, kid. War's a serious business. It's hell out there.'
BELOW: A quiet bit of relaxation with 'Vet Monthly' for Pip Torrens (Major Lawrence Brownham).

Wednesday 9 April Episode 6

An ADR session in Soho. Thank God we haven't had to do too many of these this year. Amazingly, this is my first. Thank you, Simon Okin. Quite possibly the best sound recordist in the business, he is able to get decent sound recording where other less able sound recordists would fear to tread. He'll find somewhere strategic to stick a boom or a radio mic (a small box the size of a cigarette packet), even under gun fire or the whirling blades of a helicopter. This is all a great bonus because sound that has had to be put on later always sounds like it has been added or replaced in the studio, no matter how hard they try to disguise it.

It's pathetic, but I even try to convince myself that I'm not going to notice the dubbed lines when the episode is broadcast. Most people don't notice them, but I suppose it's one of those 'not being able to see the wood for the trees' moments. After all, it's only really the trained ear of one that has experienced the ADR that does. It's like getting used to seeing yourself on screen. All you can see to begin with is you. Forget that there's a war going on, or there's a terrible storm, or that thirty other people are on the screen with you. It's 'Oh no, why did I put my hand there?', or, 'I've really got to do something about my bow legs. I look like I'm playing centre forward for the Chelsea reserves!' And I can always rely on Nige, my neighbour, friend, and DIY advisor, who's also an actor, to spot it.

THE TECHNICALITIES:

An ADR session

The idea in the studio at an ADR session is to try to match what your lips are doing. So if, like me, you're constantly 'umming' or 'urring', or breaking up your sentences with meaningful 'hums', it can be a nightmare. And sometimes, if I've been shouting the day before, and I go into the studio, the timbre of my voice can sound completely different. My voice can go from normal to 'Nightmare on Elm Street' in a matter of two or three 'Go. Go. Go.'s. Hopefully, it's just the one line or even the one word that you have to do again, but I've done a very good grunt, and lots of heartfelt sighs which have been added to scenes.

NIGE Uh oh! ADR!
ME (Unconvincingly) No. I don't think it is.
NIGE That's a definite ADR moment.
ME (Even more unconvincingly) No, really, Nige.
NIGE Get out of here. If that isn't ADR, I'm Ben Kingsley.
ME Bloody Canadian!

We're supposed to have at least ten hours off between finishing one day and starting again the next, however, on this occasion the office were quite anxious that I get there to the studio as soon as I possibly could. There was some sort of rush on. 'Any idea what it is they need me for?' 'Sorry. I just know that it's very important. And needs to be done asap.'

I arrive for the session at midday and bump in to Jo Phillips-Lane (ideal casting: Diane Keaton), who plays Karen Fitzpatrick, CSM Alan Fitzpatrick's wife. She's just finishing her session. I've not actually met Jo yet. So we introduce ourselves and have a nice little chat while they set-up for my session. It's quite bizarre how you may be doing the same job with someone and not meet them or see them for months, which is what has happened to Michelle Butterly, who plays Julie Oldroyd, and me. We met on our first day back in February. I remember it being her birthday and she had to pull me off Scot the stalker, as if she'd known me for years. 'Chris! Get off him, Chris! Leave him alone!' – I'd only just met her and I haven't seen her since.

Thursday 10 April Episode 6

Another night shoot and this is my last scene in episode 6 before two weeks off. Apparently, the dog track stuff was epic. Bigger than 'Ben Hur'. The only things that were missing were Charlton Heston and the chariots – sounds like a fifties doowop group.

Picked up at lunch time. Why so early for a night shoot? This isn't November. It's ridiculous how much earlier we seem to be called in. I know I won't be needed for hours. Someone's covering themselves all right. Usually, you get the old excuse, 'Sorry, Jonathan. I had to bring you in at this time because I'm going to need the Previa for another drop off straight away.' Twenty minutes later you walk past the Previa and there's the driver, reclining, mouth wide open, in the hard asleep position.

The scene this evening is where Chris goes to see Angela at home to have a talk about their relationship, but she's just off for a hot date with lover boy Lawrence, the Vet. It's supposed to be one of those terribly awkward and embarrassing moments that makes you cringe. I finally get to meet Pip Torrens (ideal casting: the real James Bond) who's playing the army vet, my love rival. Wicked sense of humour. We talk babies. He's due in a matter of weeks! Why is it that blokes whose partners are about to give birth sound as if it's going to be them doing it instead?

I get a bit proprietorial over Fiona. Start asking her questions like, 'What's he got that I haven't?' Fiona looks confused and says it's got nothing to do with her, it's in the script. Suddenly feel paranoid that they decided it was going to be a vet that she has a thing with. Why did it have to be a vet? That rates along side dentist, or laboratory technician. Feel this is a big blow to Chris McCleod's manhood. Is there something symbolic about a vet? Her finding attractive the man who treats the animal as opposed to her marriage to the animal in the man who is the soldier. Fiona tells me I need a holiday, and not to mention this to Annie, as they might suspect my sanity – after all, this is peak time viewing, not the Fringe.

The scene seems to take for ever. This evening, for some reason air traffic control has decided to use this normally quiet and peaceful cul-de-sac in suburban Reading as a beacon for all its long-haul jumbo jets.

All the domestic stuff this year is being filmed in the various houses that make up Byron Road in Reading. It's very 'Brookside', except Carlton hasn't bought the houses. They just rent them for the particular days they are needed. The residents are doing pretty well out of it. I've heard that its cheaper this year to do that than build sets, use a studio, or lease married quarters from the MOD. The neighbouring properties also get inconvenience compensation – if they have to have lights put up in their front gardens or massive great facilities trucks parked up on their lawns. Danger money is more of an accurate description, I feel.

THE TECHNICALITIES:

Eye-lines

Tricky eye-lines with this scene. On the doorstep. Eye-lines everywhere! Looking in. Looking out. Plus eye-lines up and down depending which doorstep you are standing on. We're all going to look cross-eyed if we're not careful. The line keeps changing for some reason. I've never been too good with this line business, but if you're not careful it can result in everyone looking in completely the wrong direction.

If I was doing a two-shot with Fiona, and we were standing directly opposite each other, you could draw a line down the middle of us, bisecting us. You could then place the camera anywhere along one of the two resulting 180-degree arcs, one on each side of the bisecting line. If you decide that you want to film the scene from my point-of-view (POV) and then Fiona's POV, which is a fairly standard thing to do as you would then have each of us speaking and reacting to the other, you would need to shoot the scene from anywhere on one of the arcs. If you were to shoot my POV on one arc and then shoot Fiona's POV from the other, you would end up with us both looking the same way, which would be very odd indeed. It gets more and more complicated the more people there are in the scene. So filming a dinner party for 12 is the equivalent of water torture for a camera crew.

Out

Friday 2 May Episode 8

First day back since 10 April. Up until 5am watching the election results. So happy, I don't feel tired. Highlight of the night was seeing Michael Portillo lose his seat. Had big lump in the throat most of the night. They did it. There is some justice after all.

New Labour. New Britain. New episode. And yet another episode being shot out of order. Fiona and I are supposed to get back together in episode 7 but it doesn't look like that will get shot before we do episode 9. So what's the state of play in episode 8?

Crispin Reece directing this episode. He came to see my play when it was on at The Donmar Warehouse in London a couple of years ago. Is it really a couple of years ago? How frightening.

This is the 'Grange Hill' episode. Filming at the Reading Blue Coat School. Lots of gorgeous nubile totty everywhere. Eyes don't know where to look. Down is probably the safest bet. I'm sure the school girls in my day weren't allowed to wear skirts the size of handkerchiefs. And why have they all got legs up to their armpits?

It's so depressing. I never thought I'd turn in to a dirty old man. Perhaps Miranda's right. It's the dirty old squaddie coming out in me.

Crispin and I talk doughnuts. I've found a man after my own heart. He feels his dependency isn't as great as mine though.

Phone call from home. Little one not well. Can't concentrate for the rest of the day. Suddenly feel this is God's punishment for drooling over teenage totty. Fortunately, my mother is able to be Florence Nightingale. M is also away rehearsing all day.

Saturday 3 May Episode 8

Picked up at 6am. Chris waiting outside – and he had already got coffee from McDonald's.

More company attacks on the school playing fields in front of all the kids. De-busing from Saracen armoured personnel carriers. Try to read election results in the back of the Saracen, while we wait for the 'go'. Don't get very far.

Meet Zoot Lynam (ideal casting: Jonathan Porritt) who plays Warren Stringer, the bully. God! I don't remember being that switched on when I was seventeen. He gives me a one-on-one ecology workshop – for most of the day. By 6 o'clock I was ready to dig a tunnel to prevent a runway. Frightening how easy it would be to brainwash me. Wish someone would brainwash me out of

LEFT: Me and that bloody beret again.

supporting Tottenham.

Friday 9 May

Episode 8

Above: Some members of the Starlight Tap Dance School, who also play rugby for Reading. Why is there always one plonker who can't resist doing the V-sign behind your head?

6am pick-up. Today we're at Reading Rugby Club (third division and semi-pro). It's a feeder club for the bigger fish, like Wasps, Harlequins and Richmond. Now, these lads from Reading Rugby Club are big, and I mean seriously big – with a capital 'B'. The scenario is that A company and B company are supposed to be playing each other in the inter-company rugby tournament. Would the King's Own Fusiliers really be able to put out teams that look like these boys? I don't think so. Surely Tom, Conor, Danny, and I are going to stick out like sore thumbs – and after a day of playing rugby with these lads it won't be just our thumbs that are sore.

The costume department has given us brand, spanking new, kit and boots. Another no no, as everyone who plays rugby knows that the kit should always have that 'washed a hundred times' look and smell of fabric conditioner. Good old Shaun, 'Master of the Jag', is a regular rugby player, and he enjoys a smug chuckle at our expense. 'Oh dear, oh dear, oh dear. Well you'll all be blistered up by lunch time.'

We rehearse, set-up, do checks (that's when someone from make-up and wardrobe come round and give you the once-over just before the camera 'turns over'), but then, wham, the heavens open up. It's difficult enough rehearsing the particular pieces of action that Crispin wants to capture without the rain as well. The first couple of hours, though, are a lot of fun.

This job has constantly thrown up situations and activities that you would have just fantasized about as a kid. Dressing up as a soldier, firing guns, and machine guns, playing rugby, winning wars .... It's always the same, though, the first few hours are great, but then gradually the novelty begins to wear off, and by mid-afternoon, it becomes just another chore. 'Let's get this thing filmed, so we can all go home.' One of the only exceptions to that which springs to mind immediately, was last year while we were filming the episode about the war against the Caravians. There was a particular scene when a few of us had to crash through a road block firing from the hip on automatic.

I would seriously have paid to do that all day. We must have shot off thousands and thousands of rounds (each round costs, I think, in the region of 50p). And a magazine containing approximately 24 rounds, being fired on automatic, only lasts a matter of seconds. 'Boys with toys,' as M says. 'Boys with toys.'

I enjoyed playing rugby at school – more enthusiasm than talent, and lots of war wounds to get girls into sympathetic mode. But sadly you simply can't play any sport, especially a contact sport, and earn your living as an actor. The risks of injury just aren't worth it. And there are often clauses in contracts that

BEHIND-THE-SCENES:

A moment of glory

The afternoon is topped off with a glorious denouement. A moment I will savour, treasure and bore future generations of Lewises with. Possibly the highlight of the series so far – for me, that is. Right up there with the back of the Land Rover scene from last year. It's a Boy's Own moment straight out of 'Ripping Yarns'.

MIRANDA Yes, all right, Jonathan. Get on with it.

Crispin, the director, decides that we need to win by not just the try, which is what it says in the script, but by a conversion instead.

EDWARD BRETT Oh, come on. Who's going to take the kick? We haven't got much time for this shot, Crispin.

CRISPIN Get one of the Reading boys up.

EDWARD Yes. But that'll mean a shot of the boot, then a separate shot of the ball, etc., etc.

(They all stand in silence. Hands on cheeks. Knotted brows. Clock ticking.)

ME I'll have a go.

(Heads swivel. Eyes stare unconvinced.)

EDWARD You sure?

ME Why not?

EDWARD Try one.

I could feel him thinking, 'Oh no. We could be here for hours.' The Reading boys are smirking. Feels like I'm about to take a match-winning kick at Twickenham. Visions of Rob Andrew's drop goal in the World Cup. 'Look at the ball and head down,' I say to myself. Bang. It whistles through the uprights. I've done it. Relief all round.

CRISPIN Right. Let's set-up for a take. We'll do this in one.

stipulate no skiing, riding, contact sports, etc. The exception which proves this rule happened to me two cricket seasons ago when M was heavily pregnant and I got smashed in the face while batting in a cricket match. She carried me in to the casualty department and initially they didn't know which of us to treat. After coming out several hours later looking like the Elephant Man with stitches holding my top lip together, I remembered I had an interview for a part on the Christmas episode of 'Casualty' the next day. I couldn't cancel it so I went along. Irony of ironies, I got the part. I think the director felt sorry for me. I don't think he could quite understand a word of what I was trying to say. But he was terribly charming and said the same thing had happened to him when he'd been playing cricket. So there you go!

In the script for today, Conor is meant to high tackle an opposing player and then get sent off. Quite achievable – on paper that is. However, the player they choose for Conor to tackle was not on paper. 'Buba' to his friends, and 'Oh shit!' to his enemies, was 6ft 7in tall. And he seemed very proud of the fact that he'd slimmed down to a ground-quaking 19 stone for his forthcoming wedding. Good luck, the future Mrs 'Buba'. And good luck Conor at 5ft 9in and 11 stone. Conor couldn't even reach Buba's neck to do the high tackle! He had to take a running jump at it, and every time he did manage to make contact with this walking wall he seemed to bounce off.

After about 11am, the day just dragged on. Getting colder and colder, standing around waiting to do these little choreographed set pieces. Rain stopping play. Conor more and more bruised.

At lunch we hear the ref's account of why he was invalided out of the police. Like many of the extras from the largely ex-service 20/20 agency he's got an incredible war story to tell. He'd been stationed at Stoke Newington in north London – all the local drug dealers, big and small had been turned over during the previous couple of weeks. One Saturday night, he and his colleague were called to a pub fight. They were the first police officers on the scene, and as they entered the pub they realised there wasn't any fight. The locals were all waiting for them – to pay the police back for their recent raids. For twenty minutes these two officers tried to fight off the gangs with no back-up. Apparently, all the possible routes to the pub had been blocked to prevent any support arriving.

Eventually, our friend the ref was dragged outside into the road. His leg was held down on the pavement and the assembled company took turns to stamp on it. His leg was shattered in many places, and mercifully he passed out with the pain. His colleague was even less fortunate. They dragged him to a broken window and ran his neck over the jagged edge.

Quite rightly, both men received hefty compensation. And while in hospital received visits from officers stationed as far away as Croydon who'd tried to make it to their assistance but had failed. There is one basic rule that police officers abide by, no matter what they think of the particular person concerned. If an officer calls for help, you do whatever you can to get there. In this instance, there was a terrible feeling of failure on the part of these other officers – that they hadn't managed to get to the scene in time. We sat listening on the meal bus, horrified and appalled.

Several of the extras who play the Fusiliers in the background of all the military bits are ex-Falklands veterans or served in the Gulf. Billy Budd is one such extra and he saw one of his best friends accidentally blow his head off on a patrol in bandit country on the Northern Ireland border, as he climbed over a fence and tripped with the Light Machine Gun. Billy was the youngest Marine who went down to the Falklands. He had his 17th birthday on Ascension Island on the way down. (He now runs his own extras agency, 'Billy's'). Our friend the ref. meanwhile has decided not to go back into the Met. What with his compensation, pension, and his new career as extra and security consultant to the stars, he says he can't afford the drop in his lifestyle. He gets us all worked up under the collar by telling us he's organising the security for the Spice Girls' forthcoming trip to the Cannes Film Festival. I ask him if he knows, by any chance, if Mel B. is a secret 'Soldier, Soldier' fan.

Saturday 10 May Episode 8

8.30am pick-up. First up is a lovey-dovey scene. Angela tells Chris she's come off the Pill. They watch TV cuddling up on the sofa. Only, of course, we aren't watching the telly – it's a pre-recorded video. We have a choice of a news item – a hamster who got trapped in the engine of a car and stayed there for days (riveting!) or the Harlem Globetrotters practising their ball skills.

The crew all prefer what's on the TV – the warm-up session for the Monaco Grand Prix. They become glued to the screen instantly. It's such a 'boyzy' sport. I don't know any woman that says, 'Oh great. The motor racing's on.' And why is it called a sport? Cars racing round a track as fast as they can go never strikes me as being sporty in the proper sense of the word. Anyway, I digress – hasn't stopped me before, I hear you saying. We plumped for the Harlem Globetrotters. There was a titter of support for the hamster. Madeleine on continuity felt it might hold some dark symbolism on an unconscious level of the McCleods' relationship. Or was it simply that the hamster piece didn't have any music in the background which made it easier from her point of view?

It's supposed to be 8.30pm and it's really 11.30am. And we have to end the scene with a snog. Now snogging, or 'the screen kiss', as far as I'm concerned is important enough to merit a Jonny Lewis tutorial. So many actors and actresses get it all wrong. And we've all seen those embarrassing, 'tongue down the throat', saliva everywhere, incidents that send you reeling back to your video machine to instantly put on a black and white with Clark Gable and Ava Gardner. Tony Curtis used to joke in the studio lot about trying to chat up the women by asking if they were going to the kissing class. And it beats me what certain directors think passes as passionate.

The most important aspect to remember in the Jonny Lewis kissing handbook, is the 'Less is More' rule. Lots of nearly kissing, as well as nose, mouth,

Above: The King's Own Fusiliers seriously consider releasing a cover version of The Village People's 'YMCA'.
Right: Some of the regular extras who make up the rest of the King's Own Fusiliers.

ear and cheek brushing, is infinitely more sensual and passionate than the tongue down throat sandwich. And this should still apply to nitty gritty, full monty, bed scenes. Lots of what I call 'nearly movements', angular and rounded not jagged and insufficient – and 'sexual sparring', rather than bottom pumping. Urgent rather than late. And don't, what ever you do, get carried away, forget who it is you're kissing and stick your tongue in their mouth. That can have dreadful consequences.

Rule number two: no garlic from 8 o'clock the night before (speaks for itself, obviously).

And rule number three: try to crack joke as soon as possible about out-of-shape body – yours, not other actor's.

My 'Soldier, Soldier' snogging career has been pretty sparse on the whole. The nearest I got to anything frisky last year was a scene with Chris getting undressed while telling Angela how he met Aoife, the mother of his long lost son. She was already in bed, mind you, extra-large T-shirt on and duvet up to her neck.

THE TECHNICALITIES:

Kissing

This year there's been a bit more on the lip-connecting front and I'm surprised at how technical it all is. 'Don't cock your head that side, you're blocking your key light.'

'Tilt your chin up, no down. No. Leave it where it is.' 'If you could just leave the minutist gap between you, because we get this lovely golden light around you.'

No getting carried away here when you've got a mark for your chin to hit – in mid-air.

I was bitterly regretting my cupcake intake over the past twenty years, and stupidly nagged Fiona for reassurance.

ME — I know I don't look great. But do you think I'm going to get away with this?

FIONA — You should have thought about that – years ago!

I knew I was right to worry about the cupcakes. Spend the rest of the time, between rehearsals and takes thrashing about doing press-up and sit-ups. Stella applies body make-up, telling me it's to take off the glare. But I know really it's to resculpture my body with clever shadow lines, to trick the audience into believing I look like I could be mistaken for a fit person.

M doesn't like seeing me do lovey-dovey stuff, understandably. Who does like to see their partner being intimate with anyone else? Voyeurs put your hands down. It's all right for you to do it, but when it comes to your partner – I know I hate seeing M doing kissing stuff. She's just told me that in the play she's rehearsing she has to do lots. Immediately picked up her script and had closer look. I don't remember that from when I read it before.

Started telling people at work it's my birthday soon. Just dropping it in casually – to jog their short-term memory. Typical conversation went like this:

ME — Oh, by the way, it's my birthday on the 20th.

ALI IN MAKE-UP (excited) Really! I'll have to make a note of that. We'll all have to go out.

ME — Yeah. That would be great. No one go to any trouble though.

Last year I kept quiet about my birthday, and it just seemed to come and go, as with everyone else's birthday. This year I thought, what the hell. If I tell people, you never know.

Told enough key people for the news to travel and I'm quite pleased with foundations for birthday spreading. Visions of a whip round and a holiday for two in Antigua, but think I could be a little over-optimistic.

Also Edward Brett's last day. He flies off to start prepping the African episode. But should see him out in Zimbabwe. The same can't be said for Adam Goodman, the second AD, who's also leaving – but he's going on to be the second AD on Spielberg's new film 'Looking for Private Ryan'.

Home early. Considered being dropped at the pub down the road, and eking out time until the end of baby duties with a few jars of ale. Then felt like a criminal for having such thoughts. Decided against the pub idea – preferring a soaking with the little one. I've always loved bath time with Abraham, he's got some great toys which I still haven't quite got the hang of, and if I haven't seen him all day, it's a joyous way to wind down – watching him have so much fun. A little bit worried, though, that me doing so much Donald Duck is going to damage him irrevocably. Will he see cartoons of DD and think that his father's a duck?

For two years, while studying at drama school, every weekend I entertained at children's parties – to keep myself. I transformed into Professor Quackers, Grand Master of the Disney Voice Laboratory. Voices and the act before tea, magic and puppets afterwards. Kids are the harshest critics, so it was a great learning curve. That's the official version – unofficially, the little bastards nearly killed me. I was never very proficient at the magic, but that wasn't always a problem as a lot of the kids already had most of the tricks I was using anyway. It wasn't encouraging, though, when I did my *pièce de resistance* rope trick to my flat mate and he turned round and said he'd seen that trick done before but this was the first time he'd actually been able to work out how it was done.

Tuesday 20 May Episode 8

Birthday today. Happy birthday me. Picked up at 5.30am by Rav. Conversation about consciousness – I think. Wasn't conscious enough to take it all in. Convinced Rav is not a real driver, but here to do a documentary on drivers or actors or something. He should be a diplomat, or reading the news. You'd believe anything he said.

Today, we're filming Alan Fitzpatrick's birthday party in the local pub. Very appropriate. Perhaps the news did filter through, after all, and filming the birthday party on my birthday wasn't just coincidental. Wait for Chris Gascoyne. He's had a relapse with the time thing. Don't mention the birthday. Hoping he might first. Silence for most of the M3. Perhaps it's all part of my birthday conspiracy, and they really have got something planned and intend to wind me up for most of the day. I start to imagine a vast cake being wheeled onto the set on the dolly, by the grip, and who it is that's going to burst out of the cake. Am I important enough for it to be Annie?

There is a lot of hanging around, disguised as a fight rehearsal as the ideas for the scenes in the pub are chat, karaoke, and punch-up – in that order. There's a lot to get through today. And this is the first time in the series so far that I will have done a scene which includes Jo Phillips-Lane who plays Karen Fitzpatrick.

For some reason, Jason White, the stunt and fight co-ordinator, has hired midgets as stuntmen for the fight. That is a slight exaggeration, of course, but they are short arses like us. All the main actors, apart from the towering lighthouse that is James Cosmo, are between 5ft 8in and 5ft 10in tall. These stunt guys even make us look big. But I assume

BEHIND-THE-SCENES:

An aside

Why is it that all the military and ex-military personnel I speak to claim not to watch the series, because 'the real thing just isn't like that'? And then they turn round five minutes later and suddenly do a, 'Do you remember the episode when... ?' moment. I love catching them out. 'I thought you said you never watched the series?' 'Oh I might catch it occasionally. It's my wife who's the big fan.' Rubbish! They love it. They love sitting there, picking holes in it.

that is the idea, whereas I would have thought in this instance, it would have been more flattering to us if the stunt guys had been of James Cosmo proportions. It would have looked like, 'we don't care how big you are – we'll still take you on.'

ABOVE: The karaoke night in the pub. Tom, Chris, Sarah, Lee and me, a.k.a. Ginger Spice, Spice-E, the Spice Twins and Old Spice.

Fortunately, I haven't had to do any shower scenes this year – that's when they always find the biggest guys possible to stand next to you; the fittest, leanest hunks who just by chance also happen to be underwear models as well. Now that's when they should be using midgets, or at the very least overweight, unfit actors like us.

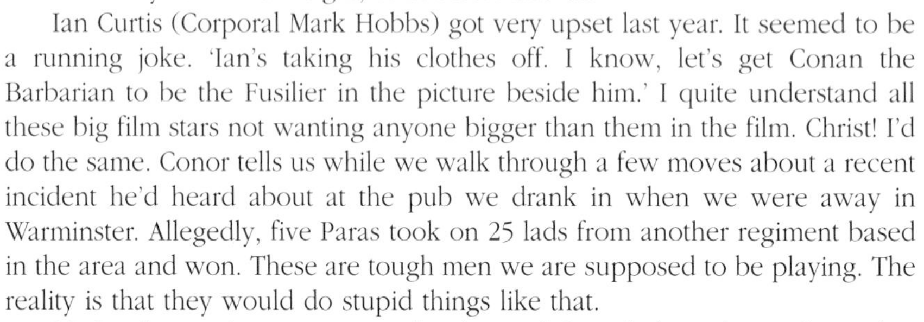

Ian Curtis (Corporal Mark Hobbs) got very upset last year. It seemed to be a running joke. 'Ian's taking his clothes off. I know, let's get Conan the Barbarian to be the Fusilier in the picture beside him.' I quite understand all these big film stars not wanting anyone bigger than them in the film. Christ! I'd do the same. Conor tells us while we walk through a few moves about a recent incident he'd heard about at the pub we drank in when we were away in Warminster. Allegedly, five Paras took on 25 lads from another regiment based in the area and won. These are tough men we are supposed to be playing. The reality is that they would do stupid things like that.

It's hard sometimes to get my head round the whole violence thing altogether, being so anti that myself. I'm sure I've pleaded 'artistic immunity' every time there's been a hint of that sort of nonsense. Nothing ever really gets settled in a fight. That's what I don't understand. But if you train men to kill, then I'm afraid you can't expect them to go for a night out and not to get involved in fighting. Perhaps they should send all soldiers to drama school so that they learn how to pretend to get violent.

Jason's getting a bit frustrated. Chris and Tom are involved in another scene, so we can't really rehearse the whole thing properly. It's such a free-for-all brawl that we all need to know exactly what we're doing, so without them it's proving difficult.

Jason always puts a lot of preparation time into the stunts – it's vital considering the lack of time he often has when it actually comes to filming them. He's learnt the paramount importance of safety from bitter experience on a stunt that went wrong on the Patrick Bergin 'Robin Hood' film. It's got to be safety first every time, and that suits me fine. Jason actually doubled for Patrick Bergin when Bergin went down with a mystery illness and couldn't film for a couple of weeks. Apparently, for much of that time the crew didn't even know it was Jason and not Mr Bergin himself, and if you imagine Jason in a black beard and wig it's not hard to see why. Mind you, put a blonde wig and a blue suit on him and I'd believe he was Margaret Thatcher.

We do the unexpected arrival of Rossi and Barton at the party first. They have gate-crashed the party with a huge pink elephant, which you just know is going to be the star of the whole bloody episode when it comes out in the autumn. The pink elephant is supposed to be discovered in Barton's locker –

planted, I think, by Rossi and discovered by the CO during an important inspection of the barracks. I assumed from the script a cuddly pink elephant the size of a normal teddy bear. Oh no – nothing so subtle. This elephant is at least five feet tall. It practically needs a crash helmet to ride on the back of Rossi's motorbike with him and Barton and it looks even more like one of the Banana Splits than Tom does.

At lunch time, I'd assumed they were all going to do the 'Happy Birthday' bit. But lunch time came and went. I convinced myself they were all feigning disinterest brilliantly, and that it had all been planned for tea time. I kept looking at the banners hanging up in the pub where we were filming. 'Happy Birthday Alan' was written up everywhere; perhaps on the other side they've got 'Happy Birthday Jonathan', and they're going to whip them round on the nod from one of the conspirators. I examined the cake which had 'Happy Birthday Alan' written in icing on the top and hoped the cake they'd bought for me looked a whole lot nicer than that one. I thought they were all doing so well keeping such a big secret from me for so long.

The sad fact is that tea time came and went and I knew then that no one had remembered, no one was even interested. The more pressing news was that they were running late and there was still the fight to do – which in the end was a bit chaotic and I felt very glad that we had that time earlier in the day to at least practise something. Graham, the director, decided he wanted the fight to look more like a bundle. Less 'set piecey' and more disorganised. Suddenly we were having to change big moves very quickly, with Robert Fabbri, the first AD, breathing down everyone's necks.

Robert (ideal casting: Ian Carmichael with a dash of George Sanders and a light sprinkling of Peter Sellers) was a second AD for nearly half the series last year. And I really enjoyed his very own brand of humour. 'Excellent' in the words of Fabbri always became 'excrement'. You'd always hear the Fabbri drone from inside his Portacabin office, and many a conversation would end with the rubbing of the hands and a double helping of 'excrement, excrement', or if you're staying overnight, it's 'Bring your smalls.'

One of the problems of the original choreography of the fight was that I needed to end up more bruised – in the original rehearsals I'd come out of it as a psychopathic bully leaving my assailant hunched over in the foetal position. Madeleine, 'Oh Continuity Madeleine' (there should be an old Irish folk song called that so you can sing it heartily when you're blind drunk on a Friday night), dear Madeleine, went up to Graham, and reminded him that in the next scene we see McCleod being patched up by Angela. And the way we were doing it looked like I would have been done for attempted murder at the very least. 'You're right,' said Graham. 'Change it immediately.' And off he went to the monitor to check something else which he didn't quite like the look of. So that when it came to the actual shot – there was me doing my impression of a punch bag. Much better said Graham. Much better.

'And how symbolic,' I retorted – which raised an eyebrow from Graham (I was flattered) and a, 'what?' from Fiona. Shortly after, I was finally given the all-clear to go home, which is called 'wrapped'. I turned round and started to say very loudly, which got the attention of all the crew who were setting up the final shot of the day, what

THE TECHNICALITIES:
A set-up
Every time you do a different shot it is called a set-up. For example, moving from a 'two shot' (a shot involving two actors) to a 'dirty single' (a close-up on one actor but in which you still see the shoulder, or a bit of the head, of the other actor) is two set-ups.

stingy arseholes they all were for forgetting my birthday, but before I could get the whole of 'birthday' out, I was being pushed out of the pub by Martin, the third AD.

MARTIN I'm sorry, Jonathan. If you could do that outside. We have got one more set-up before we can go home, and we would like to crack on with it.

What utter ignominy! Ignored, and then thrown out. I told the boys and girls of the cast I was going home to have a beer in front of the TV, as Miranda was performing tonight, and I had to baby-sit. I really wanted to rub it in and make them feel terrible. They all had long faces, and were doing great 'concerned' acting. They tried to make me go out with them for a beer. And for just a moment I glimpsed the throbbing surprise party – that they hadn't planned.

The evening was salvaged from utter disaster, though, by a lovely and intimate surprise birthday dinner at a restaurant in Waterloo called The Fire Station – with our best friends Abi and Nige, and organised by M for after her show. Felt very important when they laughed as I arrived. Heads turned. Whispered questions were asked. 'Do I know him?' 'Is he famous?' And I had great fun making a very public display of opening my presents – some rare and beautiful wind chimes for the garden from M, which now hang outside my shed where I do all my writing, and an optimistically fashionable Ben Sherman shirt from Abs and Nige.

BEHIND-THE-SCENES:

My birthday shirt

Wore the Ben Sherman. Seemed to cause a stir.

CHRIS That's a nice shirt, Jon.

ME Cheers. It's a Ben Sherman.

CHRIS I know.

(Silence)

CHRIS How come you're wearing a Ben Sherman?

DANNY Aren't you old enough to be Ben Sherman's dad?

ME It was a birthday present.

TOM Oh yeah. How was your birthday?

ME OK. No thanks to you lot.

Thursday 22 May Episode 9

Picked up at 10.45am by Rav. Receive a tutorial on the 'Fourth Dimension'. Rav talks about a Guru in India who, if you hold his hand, can flash images in your mind of major battles that occurred where you're standing hundreds of years ago – he's that switched on to the Fourth Dimension.

I try to tell the others at work what Rav has so carefully and patiently explained to me. Can't cope with hecklers, so give up after first question. Didn't know what I was talking about either so just as well there were hecklers. Conor asks if I hold his hand, could he have a flash of my performance? Don't you find times like these so annoying – when you want to try to impress your friends and colleagues with your earnest interest in something other than football, and they just don't let you.

The first scene we're filming today is a tricky one to shoot as there is so little space to work in. It's in Chris and Angela's bedroom and Angela is massaging his neck and shoulders after a hard day at work and they are having a quiet chat. It's a nice tender scene. I so rarely get to show the softer side of Chris, and I really enjoy these calmer, more intimate scenes with Fiona. I always feel I'm in a safe environment when I'm working with her. We always suggest things, and change things and constantly try to make it better.

When you film in real people's houses, you can't suddenly take a wall down, which is actually what's required here. You could in a studio, but somehow I think the owner of this particular house would be a bit upset if the crew suddenly ripped out the one wall. It means the camera can't get as low as

Jamie, who's operating it, would like.

Jamie (ideal casting: François Truffaut blended in with goujons of David Bailey, and a dollop of Oliver Tobias [the smoothie from 'The Stud', that Joan Collins classic]) has been working on and off on this series for some months now. He's had plenty of experience working on 'Soldier, Soldier' – operating the camera on at least two previous series. He's going off shortly to do a few Ruth Rendells in Dorset, and will be sorely missed as he's a brilliant camera man – always so aware of the artistic as well as the technical aspects of his job. If you get the nod from Jamie after you've filmed a scene, you know you're doing OK.

I'm lying on the bed, and Fiona is sitting on my back, massaging me – God it was a tough day at the office today! Jamie wanted to bring the camera in quite low and track along the length of the bed. Laying a short piece of track like that doesn't take very long and Dave Draper, the grip who's responsible for the dolly which the camera is mounted on, sprays all the working parts as there is an irritating little squeak coming from somewhere on the dolly or possibly the track.

Obviously, any extraneous noise from humming lights or squeaking dollies is a complete no no, and we have to wait terribly quietly while Simon Okin and Dave find the offending noise. There are so many of us in this tiny bedroom that it's like being in a World War Two submarine at the bottom of the sea waiting for the destroyer to pass overhead. I begin to get a bit self-conscious – I'm clad in only my boxer shorts after all. Fiona is told that her eye-line to the back of my head is taking her eyes too low and that she should take an eye-line twelve inches higher.

FIONA So you want me to take my eye-line to the metal step on the side of the dolly?

GRAHAM That's correct.
(Pause)

ROBERT FABBRI Turnover.

SIMON OKIN Sound.

ROBERT And action!

GRAHAM And don't forget to be sexy.

FIONA Graham, I'm afraid I'm finding it very hard to be sexy to a metal step.

ROBERT Cut! Reset please. We will be going again.

The bed is put on legs. Suddenly it looks like an Elizabethan four-poster with all the lamp stands around it. It does the trick and Fiona is now able to use the infinitely more attractive eye-line of the back of my head. Unfortunately, because of all the faffing around, we have now gone over the official wrap time. Robert stands in a huddle with Graham chewing the top of his walkie talkie aerial, and shaking his head. All I manage to catch is Robert's final compromise, 'Well, ten minutes then, and

BEHIND-THE-SCENES:

Creating the atmosphere

Sometimes you have to act with people doing intimate stuff and they don't give much back. You can always tell by the eyes – what's going on in the eyes. Sometimes, when you realise that there is actually very little going on behind the eyes you have to do it all yourself. By that, I mean you have to summon up all the emotion that your character is supposed to be feeling without the necessary input from the other person in the scene with you. It can be horrible. Because of the technical restrictions, you might have to do some very emotional dialogue looking straight at a lamp stand, or the side of a camera, because there's no room for the other actor to be where they would really be in the scene. The eye-line has to be cheated round so that the audience see a pair of eyes, or at least one eye instead of a chin or a nose. And it's always very important to the other actor you're working with in the scene, when it's your turn to give your lines from off-camera, ie when it is their close-up, to really do it at performance level. You sometimes hear stories of very unprofessional behaviour from actors, who once they have done their close-up, suddenly relax, and forget their lines or stop concentrating, which can obviously be very difficult for the other actor. I've even heard stories of arrogant stars who decide not even to be there for their off-lines.

they'll have to do it in one take.' Thank you Graham. At least he stuck his neck out for us – all we have to do is not let him down. So no pressure then. No pressure at all. One take – that's all we're going to get. Gulp!

The crew reset as we have a quick walk-through the scene. I wouldn't even call it a rehearsal. At the same time as we walk through it, we're getting changed. Well, Fiona's getting changed, I'm just getting dressed. Trying to remember the lines. It's me who's got the bulk of the dialogue. In these situations I sometimes panic. I think part of me wants to shoot myself in the foot. If only to say, 'There you are, you see. You couldn't do it. When the pressure was on you bottled out.' I had to will myself to remember the lines and keep in the right position so that we both stayed in the frame. But one take? Some directors, and actors for that matter, swear that the first take is usually the best take – for the acting at least. Often, of course, you're buggered up by circumstances beyond your control – the boom comes into shot, or the camera can't hold you in the frame if you stand up or sit down too quickly.

The complete opposite of that is Stanley '2001' Kubrick who is famed for his hundreds of takes on each shot, trying to get the perfect take where the actors are so natural in front of the camera that the camera no longer feels like the intrusion that it inevitably is.

GRAHAM Right. Let's shoot the rehearsal.
ME But then it's not a rehearsal.
GRAHAM Yes it is. We're just going to shoot it that's all.
ME I thought you wanted to do this all in one take.
GRAHAM I do.
ME So is this a rehearsal or a take?
GRAHAM It's a rehearsed take.

We actually did it – without forgetting our lines or bumping into the furniture, as they say. And I couldn't believe it once the take was over. 'Right, that's a wrap,' shouted Robert on his walkie talkie. I jumped in very quickly. I knew I could do it better.

'Please could we just do one more. One more. Please.' There was silence. The crew looked horrified. Simon Okin had already half packed the sound gear away. But I felt I had to do this. After all, it's going to be me up there being scrutinised by 11 million viewers, not them. Graham had a tough decision to make. Often actors ask to do one more take – out of insecurity more than anything else. But, and this is a gross generalisation, I think given the choice, most actors would prefer to do one more take as opposed to one less. The next one might always be 'the one'. It very rarely is, though. And this was the decision that Graham had to make. Was I simply being insecure about the take? Surely it was fine, and we didn't need to go again, or did I really warrant another go at it?

We clocked each other for a few seconds. I mouthed over the heads of all the other people in the way that I felt there was one point in the last take where I suddenly felt outside the performance. I felt self-conscious and too aware of the camera being on me. It's always a difficult balance because part of you always has to be aware of the medium – where your light is, or a boom

RIGHT: Paul Brown with Danny and Chris

right under your nose, or even the whirring of the film going round in the camera when it is a very quiet bit – and this can sometimes jolt you out of your character for a moment and remind you that it's a film and not real. It's that moment that I think can sometimes be detected in the eyes of an actor on the screen.

Getting back to Graham, though, he very kindly gave me the benefit of the doubt. As a rule, I haven't let him down, or cried wolf, so I think he knew that I was genuinely worried about the last and only take and so he nodded to me and in his most authoritative directorial voice he told everyone, 'One more everybody. We will be going again.' I thanked him, and tried to block out the moans and groans of those around me.

Fiona and I looked at each other, checked a couple of little details, and then we were off again. The 'cut' seemed to be forever coming, but when it was finally uttered it was worth it. The take was far superior to the one before, and everyone knew it. Simon Okin came up and whispered in my ear, 'That was good. You did the right thing.' I felt exonerated, but most of all I felt relieved. The pressure had been enormous. I looked down and my hands had started to shake. From the setting-up to the final 'cut' on that scene had lasted exactly 15 minutes. I was shattered. I'd certainly earned my twenty quid that day.

BEHIND-THE-SCENES:

Visualisation

After this morning's 6am pick-up, Rav tried to get me to do 3-D visualisation.

RAV Try to think about your flat – all of it, from no particular vantage point.

ME But how do you visualise something without it being from a particular vantage point?

RAV All right. Think of it from every vantage point at once.

ME Rav! It's six in the morning.

RAV That's a very traditional concept of time you're using. Now, think of it like a transparent paperweight – the ones that you shake up and they snow, or a glass of water. I know you're an actor, but don't tell me you've got a problem imagining the inside parts of a transparent paperweight or a glass of water?

(Silence as I visualise snow falling inside my flat which is now full of water.)

RAV There you are.

ME What?

RAV Now you're getting close to a higher-dimensional experience.

(All I can see is Karl standing in the kitchen, holding our yellow bucket and shaking his head. Karl's our plumber. Decide not to tell Rav that.)

ME Right. Well, I'll visualise in 3D till we get there Rav.

Friday 23 May Episode 8

Nice surprise after the ignominy of Tuesday. At lunch time, Fiona came onto the coach where we eat. She'd bought a cake and a bottle of champagne. I took it all back about them, and went round like a terrible old 'luvvie' kissing everyone and thanking them. Must have looked pretty sick – men in uniform kissing each other. Kissed the girls as well, mind. Kissed anyone I could – wishing them a happy New Year, or happy birthday. Must be all the champagne. Feeling pissed. Now I know why they don't get champagne for everyone's birthday. They'd never get any work done in the afternoons. Reminds me of the film I worked on in Poland last year.

You got to work in the morning, and you were offered vodka – no, thank you. You sat down in a chair ten minutes later and you were offered vodka – no, thank you. It came to elevenses – and there were no sticky buns. It was, would you like some more vodka?

I had to have some in the end – I'd carry a cup of it round all day with me, just to stop them asking. For most of the time I think I must have been in a drunken haze, and I'm sure my speech on the film was just a little bit slurred. Mind you, so was everyone else's. It's a very slurry language anyway, is Polish. Lots of 'Mooosh' and 'svvzzzdz.' It's surprising how quickly I just accepted what was considered the norm out there. I'd never dream of having a drink at lunch time while working over here. I can't drink during the

THE TECHNICALITIES:

Working your way up

Sophia (ideal casting: Naomi Campbell with a brain), who is the clapper loader, is on the up, and it's her responsibility to look after all the film stock, marking it all, and making sure everything is in its right place. Sometimes she may pick up a bit of focus pulling experience if we have a second camera out filming at the same time. The DOP, either Peter Greenhalgh (ideal casting: Alan Ladd) or Chris Howard, would operate the second camera and she would pull focus. This is the next rung on the ladder, and you can spend years as a focus puller, before someone gives you a chance to actually operate. Focus pulling and operating are very pressurised jobs. As Dermot the focus puller says, 'You can be sure that if the rushes came back from two days filming and they weren't in sharp focus or the picture was wobbly, the euphemistic P45 would be on the car windscreen before you could say "wrap".'

If an actor, on the other hand, was having problems with a character, the actor, as long as they weren't downright bad, would have more leeway than two days in finding his or her performance. It's much harder to define an interpretational skill than an absolute one. Either you can follow an actor walking along and keep him or her in sharp focus or you can't. How you think the actor is playing the scene is far more difficult to judge.

day, whatever – one pint and I need to sleep it off till four.

And the Polish crew couldn't believe they had to work every day. It was such a culture shock for them. Polish crews are paid for the job, rather than weekly. So they get a percentage of their salary at the beginning, a percentage in the middle of filming, and the rest at the end. And what tends to happen is that the director will turn up to the set where they are filming and he might not like the light that particular day, so everyone gets sent home again and there's no filming on that day. Consequently, a film that should take only a few months to film could take nearly a year. So they loved working for the Welsh production company that I was working for, because they would be expected to work every day. There was none of this going home business because of the light, etc. And it meant that they would be able to move onto something else sooner and make their money quicker than they had been banking on.

Jonathan (ideal casting: Tim Henman), the camera trainee, tells me it's his birthday today. He hadn't made a big fuss like me. He tells me he got over that stage in his life when he was twelve. I don't rise to him though. Instead, I tell him if that's the case then he can't have any of my champagne, and I won't be his friend any more – so there!

Jonathan has just finished at film school and is now building up those all-important credits, experience, and network of potential employers, which is how the technical side of the film and tellyvision business seems to work. So and so knows so and so, or worked with a mutual friend or colleague and they can't do the job, so recommend someone else they know or have worked with. And so it goes on. Members of the crew don't seem to have agents like actors do, although directors and designers often do.

It's extremely annoying having someone else called Jonathan on the same set, because every time the name is spoken – often shouted from great distances in a 'do this now' kind of voice – I leap onto my feet and look as if I've done something terribly naughty or something that I shouldn't, and really it's the other Jonathan who's being called for.

Saturday 24 May Episode 8

Picked up 6am. The topics of conversation this morning between Rav and me were 'The Sweeney' and 'Bodyguards'. General thumbs-up for the advert paying homage to, or taking the piss out of (depending on where you're coming from), John Thaw and Dennis Waterman in 'The Sweeney'.

Alison Banks' last day. Alison Banks – otherwise known as 'Highland Spice', as opposed to our other female Celt icon, Fiona, otherwise known as 'Khaki Spice'. We're going to sorely miss Alison who's off to work on 'Thief

Takers'. She has been a lovely second AD – even though she does chew gum for Scotland and wears bright orange flared leggings. Ditto Jamie Harcourt, camera operator and Robert Fabbri, first AD – not that they chew gum for Scotland or wear bright orange leggings – although what they do in their own time is their business. I'm talking about the fact that Jamie is off to Dorset to do his Wexford mysteries and Robert is also going on to 'Thief Takers' – in his new-found first AD role.

Just found out that Fiona has been out with Roy who's head of the wardrobe department and the only person, apart from Annie T (producer), who's done all seven series of Soldier. Give those old campaigners a medal. She's been out with Roy to choose some nice Civvy clothes. I wondered why she hadn't been complaining so much recently. And she managed to keep her little shopping jaunt so quiet. She was probably terrified that if we found out we'd all be booking our afternoons with Roy in Oxford St and the King's Road. It's much easier for Fiona to arrange a shopping trip in town because she has to commute from Glasgow, where she lives. So when she works, she comes down for several days at a time, staying at the hotel, and then when she's finished she either flies or takes the train back to Glasgow. So she often has the odd morning or afternoon to do that kind of thing. Conor also commutes, but from Dublin. And it's bizarre to think that it's quicker for him to commute from Dublin than for him to live in Bristol, for example, or Manchester.

Above: Alison Banks (aka Highland Spice) smiles a farewell smile outside one of the caravans.
Top: 'Which way does this webbing go again?', quizzes Ben Nealon ... 'How many years have you been doing this show?', replies Keith, from wardrobe.

ABOVE: Real soldiers watching the pretend ones.

I can't believe it, but today I'm in very early because of rain cover and when I left the house there wasn't a cloud in the sky. It was a beautiful summer morning. That's another great excuse that is wheeled out, if you ever question the decision to bring you in six hours too early, especially when you look up and there isn't a cloud to be seen.

Finally get to do my bit with Ben Nealon (Captain Jeremy Forsythe). It's right at the beginning of the episode and we're watching the boys abseil down the side of a building. I get to hold a megaphone and do stupid things with it – like Donald Duck impressions. Never heard DD out of a megaphone before, don't think I want to again.

At the Army School of Catering in Aldershot. Signed lots of autographs. Lots of what seem like very young recruits who are doing catering courses watch the filming all morning. I think I'd prefer to watch paint dry, though they did get to see a bit of abseiling and Ben, of course. Some of the female recruits look like they'd like to abseil down Ben!

This is Ben's last year. He's served four years on the series and come up from a fresh-faced Sandhurst graduate to a rugged and wrinkled Company commander. He knows now that somehow he's going to end up back in Africa after the Zimbabwe episode. It'll be interesting to see how that story line pans out.

I think I've taken over from James Callis this year as the rain cover king. The amount of times James came in last year and wasn't used was extraordinary. James played Major Tim last year. But I suppose they've got to do it, because if it is raining outside and they can't film, they've got to be able to have an interior scene as an alternative – otherwise the crew would pretend they were all Polish and go home early. Where's it all going to lead? I wonder if they know themselves in the office yet. Perhaps they're rolling the dice even as I write this to see which of us is going to be the mandatory casualty of the series. Blown-up? Shot? Blown-up and shot? Blown-up after being shot? The possibilities are endless. And I've just been told a little secret which I believe has been running for a number of series now – the character who appears in the drum in the opening credits is the character who's going to be meeting a sticky end. I don't know whether this tradition will continue with this series – probably not now that I've mentioned it. I must get hold of some videos of previous series and find out if it's true.

Had a nice chat in the afternoon with Major Claude Davidson RGR, who's been attached to the unit now for a few months as the official military advisor. He's with the Gurkhas. Robin Cope doesn't seem to be around very much at the moment, but they tend to get him in for the more hands-on, rolling-up-the-sleeves-and-getting-down-in-the-dirt kind of military advice. Major Claude is more the 'do as I say not as I do', check shirt, Hush Puppies and Labrador type of adviser. A trouble shooter as opposed to a rifle shooter. He's been serving for over twenty years.

The road to Damascus

Tuesday 27 May Episode 7

6am pick-up. Angela and Chris are now reconciled after their on off, on off, off, off, off relationship. But we don't film the scene until Thursday where Angela comes to tell Chris she wants him back. That gives production at least 24 hours to cut a scene – so anything can change before then. Perhaps they might re-write the scene where Angela comes to find Chris in his room at the Sergeants' Mess, and he won't be there after all. He's gone fly fishing with Butcher. The scene today is us saying goodbye to Hobbs, who's leaving the Army, but he doesn't get to do his confrontation with Colonel Drysdale which pre-empts this until next Friday.

This is my first day with Chris King directing. I'm a bit nervous as I want to make a good impression, bearing in mind the high regard the other guys have for him. It turns out that Chris and I have a mutual friend and colleague – Bruce Alexander, who plays David Jason's boss in the 'Inspector Frost' series. I know Bruce from a company called ACTER. Bruce is one of the associate directors of ACTER – a company originally started back in the seventies by a number of distinguished actors from the RSC and an academic called 'Murph' from the University of California, Santa Barbara. Five actors do an entire Shakespeare play, doing all the parts, and with minimal costume and props. They are travelling players in the true sense of the word – spending a week's residency at each college or university in the USA, teaching and performing as they go. Chris knows Bruce because they were at university together. Now I'm wondering what Bruce might have said about me. 'Nice bloke, shame about the acting', or maybe, 'nice acting, shame about the bloke.' I try to discern one or the other from our handshake and exchange of pleasantries.

We spend almost the whole day sitting around two tables in the pub as Chris shoots what is quite a long dialogue scene from lots of different angles. At the end of it, Butcher has to find a winning chocolate bar wrapper (it's a holiday to Disney World), only to have the girl who works behind the bar pick it up and, thinking it's rubbish, accidentally throw it on the fire. It's terrible for the eye-lines as we're all sitting for much of it and the line keeps changing. It would be so much easier if they could lay a 360-degree track all around the table for the camera. Maybe if this was a movie, they would have done.

It's a beautiful day outside and we're stuck inside under the even warmer

RIGHT: The 'B' camera crew with clapperboard.

lights. Cables everywhere, extras everywhere, my performance everywhere. Only got two lines all day – rest of the time is spent snogging Angela – or nearly snogging as we sit being watched at the table by the rest of the boys. Seems a bit insensitive to Hobbs really; as he's drowning his sorrows and lost army career while we do more kissing and making-up than Romeo and Juliet. However, that's the way it's written.

We all have to go and sit outside as much as possible because it's just too stuffy inside. Danny and Caroline have a busy and even warmer time having to stand in for us today. Caroline's predecessor, Sarah, has been another casualty to the 'Thief Takers' camp and I am missing my photographic assistant. She's been a big help on the snapping front, when I've been tied up in a scene and haven't been able to do the photographing.

Thursday 29 May Episode 7

1.15pm pick-up. Miranda filming an episode of 'The Bill'. She stayed over in Waterloo at a friend's place to get a decent night's sleep before heading off for 'The Bill's base in Merton.

Found baby-minding somewhat time-consuming and finally had ten minutes to get dressed at midday when his Majesty went down for his mid-morning nap. Felt like joining him, but had to keep awake because my Mum was due to look after him any minute and I didn't want her to ring the bell. Kept eagle eye out. If this is what baby duties do to me, how would I cope if I was having to do this full time?

Get to work and told that my scene with Fiona – scene 47 – is now cut. What did I say? What did I tell you diary? I knew it. According to Madeleine's timings, the episode is running approximately ten minutes over and the whole script is being trimmed.

BEHIND-THE-SCENES:

A Steadicam shot

A Steadicam shot is a great way of filming an action scene. Steadicam is what you see on 'ER' or 'NYPD Blue'. The camera gets right in there with the actors and it is constantly moving – it helps to create a real sense of energy and tension. Occasionally, if the Steadicam gets a bit carried away, then the onset of dizziness and sea sickness has only to be a matter of time. However, I'm not knocking Steadicam. Hell, I'd film everything with Steadicam. Imagine 'Coronation Street' filmed with a Steadicam, or 'Family Fortunes'.

The Steadicam is a camera which, by a miracle of technology, is mounted on a frame worn by the camera operator. This means that he and the camera are totally mobile. There are very few of these around in this country, and they are incredibly expensive to hire. The operators tend to look like Olympic athletes, because of the weight of the camera. So the director would really have to justify the need to hire one for a specific scene – usually they tend to get used on 'Soldier, Soldier' for action sequences.

RIGHT: Another series, another war. In the last series, we leapt from our wrecked helicopter and the ensuing action was all filmed by a Steadicam. Last year the Regency Islands, this year Zokindi.

BELOW: The Steadicam strapped to a strapping camera operator with Dermot pulling focus on the move.

Last year in the war episode we did a 200 metre dash from our crashed helicopter into the woods which was all filmed with the Steadicam following us. I'd never done anything like that before, and we spent most of the day rehearsing and practising the route through the trees – which tree we had to get to and by when – and the Steadicam had to keep five of us in its frame all the time. Some of the trees had what's called 'squibs' attached to them – these were little explosions which were there to look like enemy gunfire hitting the trees. I nearly blacked out after doing the take three times, but the Steadicam operator was ready to jog up Mount Everest.

It just so happens that the scene is first on the list. Why is it that every time they seem to need a cut it comes out of Chris's story line with Angela? We're certainly taking the hint all right. There are now so many holes in the story line, it's hard to see the bits in between. Today, we did the scene where Angela arrives on Chris's doorstep in the Sergeants' Mess with two suitcases and she wants him to move back in with her.

The scene that was cut followed on from there and only happened to be the crux of their whole on-off relationship for the entire series so far. In the scene, Angela tells Chris that she has realised she can't be without him after trying to sleep with Lawrence the vet. So now the audience will be left with the reconciliation but none of the explanation. That's left to their imagination. Even then, there was no mention of Aoife or Chris's son Liam, or Angela's acceptance of Liam, which is what real people would talk about in this situation.

This was my last domestic scene with Fiona in the series. It made me feel sad.

On a brighter note, visa forms for Zimbabwe have to be filled in tonight. Still can't quite believe that we are going. Still convinced it's a huge conspiracy and that we're going to be filming in Zimbabwe, south of Guildford.

It's been hotter today than it'll probably get in Zimbabwe. Isn't it sad I can't even get to go to Africa at the right time. It'll be their winter when we get there, so although it might get into the high seventies during the day, at night we've been warned it can get very cold. So much for sitting out on the veranda, pretending to be Stewart Granger with a rum punch looking at the stars and the elephants.

It was so hot today, that they had to switch some scenes around. There was too much glare from the sun to film outside, so they had to do some interior scenes first until it calmed down. I wonder if they had to bring any of the actors into work especially for 'sun cover' or 'glare cover'. That's a first. It ranks up there with leaves on the line, or the wrong kind of snow.

BEHIND-THE-SCENES:

A conspiracy

Rav tells me the story of the conspiracy theory surrounding the moon landings and how a number of people believe the first NASA landing on the moon was actually orchestrated, like a big film, in a studio. The Americans were desperate to show the world that they got there first and beat the Russians.

SECOND AD Sorry Jonathan, we're expecting really heavy sun tomorrow so we're going to have to bring you in I'm afraid – for cover.
ME You're joking.
SECOND AD I'm really sorry. If it were up to me and all that …

Chris King also has to fit in a couple of other scenes from episode 5 that he has to re-shoot. Don't know what the problem was; it was all a bit confusing. Chris King looks incredibly calm throughout – the man never sweats. He must save a fortune in deodorant.

While we wait for final set-up Fiona tells a great story about a gallery owner she knows. He met Madonna while on business in America and she invited him out to dinner. She seemed to pay him a considerable amount of attention, and so naturally when she announced she was going dancing, he thought he'd tag along as he was beginning to fancy his chances. On the dance floor, Madonna was soon surrounded by impossibly attractive and fit looking men – it looked like the Queen bee and her workers.

The art dealer decided to muscle in, not wanting to lose out on all the

BEHIND-THE-SCENES:

An ADR session

On Friday, there was an ADR session in Soho for episodes 1 and 6.

The effects at the beginning of episode 1 look excellent, and it's a strange cocktail of the sublime and the ridiculous to think we rehearsed, worked out, rehearsed again for more than two days for what, in the end, actually turned out to be only a few minutes worth of film. And I swear I must be in just a few seconds of it. If you'd blinked you would have missed me – especially with the hat and all the gear on. I suppose that's why we're here, so that if they blend in enough sound of us shouting and grunting wary stuff underneath it might be possible to establish our verbal presence better than our visual one. It definitely looks like an advert for the army. We even look like proper soldiers – I think.

Memories of Bishopstrow House and being away from home for all that time come flooding back into my consciousness as I watch the recording. Was I really there among all that? It's huge. There are hundreds of extras. It could be a recreation of D-Day. A feeling of pride immediately surges through me to think I was part of all this. Suddenly feel very nostalgic, and experience first fillip that this job is not going to last forever. Middle of July unexpectedly leaps into the middle of next week.

ADR for episode 6 is just the one line. Two words and an exclamation mark, 'A vet!' This was actually an ad lib at the time, so I suppose it serves me right for getting carried away. I like it, though, and it sums up how Chris was feeling at that time – it's the nearest thing to being able to say, 'Oh, f***!' without actually having to say it.

Danny, Ian, and Chris are also there doing bits and pieces. At one point we all have to get up and make encouraging and wary noises for the opening action sequence of episode one. All five of us stand sheepishly at the microphone staring at the screen where the sequence is being shown. We look and sound like 'Take That' itching for a fight.

US Come on! Aaaaargh! Go. Go. Go.

A white vertical line goes from left to right across the picture and when the line reaches the right-hand side of the screen that is your queue to speak, and you have to do your best to match your own lip movements on screen. In this case, because it was general wary noise above the action, there was no specific lip synch to follow. The sequence went on for several minutes, and by the end of it we were beside ourselves. The ridiculousness of this had hit us all at roughly the same time. I think I turned into Kenneth Williams, Chris just stood coolly shaking his head – with a few 'Oh dear, oh dear, oh dears' thrown in, and Tom and Ian were watching Danny who'd turned into this bizarre character from Yorkshire he had met at the hotel one night. This chap was in his seventies and down south with his bowls team and couldn't stop swearing: 'Come on, you silly ****! I told you! Come on!'

When we've finished, Danny, Ian and Chris talk about what a good time they had the previous night. Suddenly feel very left out that I hadn't been asked along. Tom tells me he would have invited me but he knew what the answer would have been as it was such short notice. He didn't want to drag me away from my shed in the garden where he knew I was tucked away writing this diary. A mate of his was opening a bar in south London and as all the others, apart from Al Pacino, live down south it was local for them, whereas for me I would have had to get my passport out, packed an overnight bag and flown across the river. I don't know what it is about Tom and this north and south London thing. He always seems to get quite tense anywhere north of Camden, and he has to know where the nearest tube station is.

Ian announces that it's his birthday today, and Danny reveals it was his birthday a couple of days ago, but that he didn't want to say anything, and it looks like they're all meeting up tonight somewhere. Can't go. Haven't got a babysitter. M still doing play. Finishes tomorrow night. Appointment with shed more likely. Sixty thousand words at the moment may as well be 60 million. Lots to do. Photos to sort through, captions to write, etc. Anyway, going to a cousin's bar mitzvah tomorrow and taking Abe the babe while Mum finishes filming 'The Bill'. Mum turning into very busy bee. I want to be fresh for the service in the morning and the ensuing knees-up in the evening at a very posh Country Club in Hertfordshire. So going out twice in two evenings could cause the old system to overload.

Starting to see so many grey hairs – can't pull them all out or might start looking like Paul Daniels. Best policy is to ignore them and then they might go away.

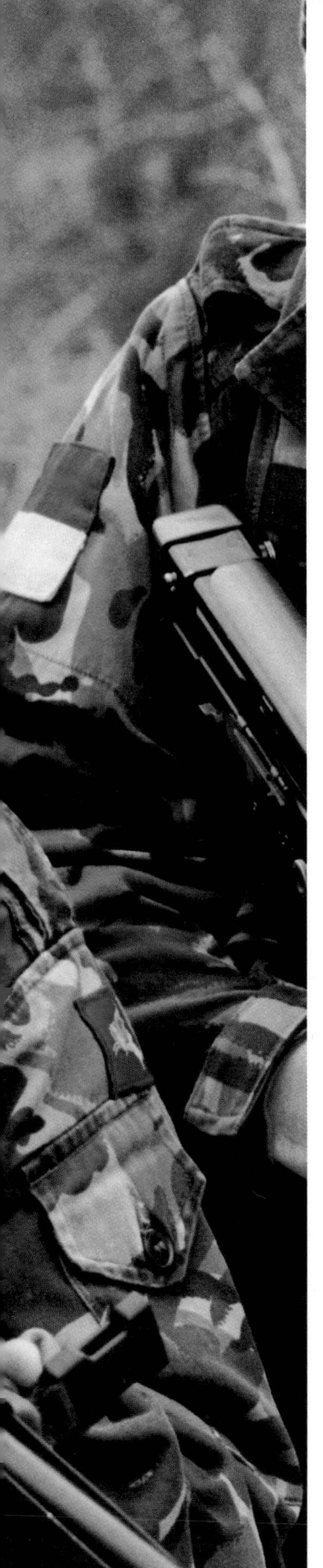

ground work he'd put in earlier. So he's dancing away (and apparently he dances like Basil Fawlty when anyone dares let him get up on the dance floor at home) and he just can't get close to Madonna at all. He pushes past muscley men on either side, but still can't get right to her. Suddenly, he's being dragged off the dance floor by two of Madonna's huge minders who explain that she isn't dancing for fun. She's auditioning dancers for her next show and this is the way she always likes to do it, and would he mind 'butting out'.

Monday 2 June Episode 7

This is my last week of filming in the UK on this current series. It's a 6am pick-up and it's all round the houses this morning as it's going to be the first time this year that all, or nearly all, the main principles are in working at the same time. Consequently it's going to be a full Previa on the way down to Hankley Common. Hankley's where we shot much of the war episode last year. It's a large expanse of training ground just off the A3 towards Portsmouth.

It's a beautiful fresh morning, and first stop after me is Ben, who sits on the metal staircase outside his pleasure dome in Islington, just off the main throb of Upper St.

Ben is never late, always reliable.

Next stop is Chris who, again, is waiting outside. Can this be correct?

Oh no. It's not. It's someone else. But this someone else also seems to be waiting for a dark grey Previa. The guy is Andy, and he turns out to be a friend of Chris's from Nottingham. They are friends from the same village, and go way back. He tells us Chris is in McDonald's getting his intravenous caffeine line set-up for the week as we're all going to be staying away.

Still can't believe that I'm going to be away for a week. It's going to be like having a holiday. M has now finished her play and 'The Bill', and is on full-time baby duties for the whole week. I'm now feeling funny about being away. I've spent a lot of time with Abe the babe over the last few weeks and we're very close at the moment. Still, at least M is going to be there for bath and bed time and her evenings aren't going to be spent being sodomised and beaten-up on stage at the Young Vic.

'Chris Gascoyne emerges from Macs and runs up road to Previa.' It looks like a shot from the movie, 'The Making of "Soldier, Soldier"'. I'm now wondering whether Chris is transforming into De Niro. Is he wriggling out of his Pacino skin and getting a pair of De Niro wings? The cigarette stuck to the side of the mouth and the delicate, yet gangster-like, square-shaped shades perched on the bridge of his nose are terribly 'Taxi Driver'. Convinced now that Gascoyne could be a movie star. He's definitely got something very moreish both on and off the screen.

Andy produces a vibrating pager from his hip and explains that his partner is about to give birth any day. Chris has got him a week's work as an extra on the show. That'll keep them in Pampers for a few weeks. He'll be playing a fusilier alongside Danny's brother who's also coming down for the week.

Next stop was picking up Ian Driver (ideal casting: John Denver, in case we decide to make 'Soldier, Soldier – the musical') who's playing Captain Somers, the exercise invigilator. He, too, is baby friendly. He hasn't been out of

LEFT: Fusilier Andy Butcher (Danny Cunningham – or is it Stan Ogden?)

his flat since his partner gave birth two-and-a-half weeks ago. He's still in nappy mode with that sleep deprived look, so doesn't really speak for a couple of hours until he readjusts to Previa time.

The sequence that we're away filming all week is for an exercise that the King's Own are mounting as preparation for their peace-keeping role in Africa. It's an operation involving us as the peace-keepers, Orange Forces as the 'enemy', and a civilian population, or 'civ pop' as they are referred to, which comprises friends and family of the King's Own. There must have been about thirty extras playing the 'civ pop'. I do love the army for abbreviations. It's like another language which excludes outsiders from gaining access. You've got your SA 80s as opposed to the old SLRs; then there's the CSM, RSM, which are not to be confused with your RMA, RGJ or your RGR.

Why is it that we spend nearly the whole day doing loads and loads of drive-by shots – up hills, down hills, approaching a road block. You name it. We could have been doing a star turn on 'Top Gear'. I can just hear Jeremy Clarkson, 'Now that Land Rover's a sight for sore eyes. I reckon the prospect of driving that little tiger into action sounds better than rubbing baby oil into the aching limbs of Moira Stewart on a bad hair day.'

The real meat of the scene, which involved us all getting out of the vehicles – or 'debussing' – to remove an obstacle blocking the road, had to be rushed at the end of the day. We all felt terribly pressured and uncomfortable because there was no time to rehearse and everyone was expecting us to get it right first time. And bearing in mind there wasn't any particular continuity for the drive-by stuff, I think they could have scheduled the road block stuff first.

I jumped down from the Land Rover at the road block, and it was quite a

Below: The Orange Forces (or, as they were affectionately called, 'The dirty dozenish'), as led by Robin Cope (second left).

dramatic leap. But Martin, the camera operator for this episode, came up to me, put his arm on my shoulder (so I knew it must be serious), and said (you have to imagine a Welsh accent for this), 'Great leap Jonathan, very dramatic – only trouble is I can't keep you in the frame if you leap eight foot into the air. So, as they say in America, "I want it big, but not ballroom."' Love it. 'Big, but not ballroom.' How can I get that into a script?

Martin's an excellent operator. He's always there with encouragement or advice. Just what the insecure actor needs (ideal casting: a Welsh Peter Duncan from 'Blue Peter', or an Aussie surfer from Bondi Beach).

In the afternoon, Cliff Kent is out on set taking stills. Cliff has been hired by Carlton to come out for a day on every episode and get those all-important stills which end up in the *TV Times*. Cliff Kent, older brother of Clark Kent (Superman), is the advert for what a stills photographer should look like (ideal casting: Cliff Robertson, Cliff Richard and Cliff Hanger all rolled into one). I had a few posed shots taken by a tree while they did a drive-by shot which was filmed over my shoulder so I didn't have to be there. One of the drivers from Action Vehicles just threw on a combat jacket and drove the Land Rover for me. It could be my shoulder, your shoulder or Tony Blair's shoulder, as far as anyone would be able to tell.

I wanted a few stills with beret off, but my scalp's been a terrible mess for the last few days – too much coffee. So not wanting to have photos of Chris posing in an Arctic snow storm, decided to have stills taken with beret on. Initial Polaroids, which Cliff always takes look OK. He'll then develop and process the negative by hand, getting rid of all those awful blemishes and making me look like Chris McCleod from 'Baywatch'. He even makes the tree look better. Tracey Whitton, the deputy picture editor from Carlton's office in Nottingham, is with Cliff, and she's very long suffering with all of us (ideal casting: Sally Field again).

ME I can't have my pictures done looking like this!

ANON I really, really, really think it would look better if I took my jacket off – and put it on my head.

ANON Can you come back tomorrow when I've sobered up?

Spoke to Helen Flint in the office about flights to 'Zim'. Helen calls it that; think I'll do the same. Sounds like she knows what she's talking about. Old seasoned traveller to Africa, and all that. Things being booked for another film being made in Zimbabwe, so Helen has just hot-footed back from buying up Harare. Also it seems that every world organisation and wildlife charity have chosen to hold a conference in Harare while we're there – so now flights and accommodation are going to be tricky.

Got to the hotel about eight. Knackered. It's been a long day. Had a Jacuzzi in the bathroom – excellent. After a few minutes turned it off. Felt guilty that I was having too much fun. Also worried it was making too much noise. There you are – typical behaviour from Jewish son. Guilt driven the whole time. Told everyone about the Jacuzzi in the bar when I went for a drink afterwards, they're all fuming. Good!

Did some homework on the scenes for tomorrow. Daren't examine it too closely or I'll have too many unanswered questions. Best just to get lines under belt and sense of direction the whole scene is going in – leave details for tomorrow.

Tuesday 3 June Episode 7

The early night last night wasn't so early after all. Went to bed around 2ish. Up at 6.30am. But the location is just five minutes from here. The only high note is that the others look even worse than me.

For some reason I'm one of the first into make-up this morning – even before the girls, who take much longer, obviously.

My tattoo only takes about twenty minutes to put on, and I'm not even sure whether it'll be seen today, but they've got to do it, just in case. It's of a winged Pegasus, which is one of the emblems of the Airborne Forces and it's been carved onto an ink pad which is then put straight onto my left forearm, between two very prominent moles, and then gone over with a very sharp, dark grey, eye-liner pencil.

There is a bit of Latin underneath 'Ad Onum Omnes', which translated means 'Death from above'. Unfortunately, sometimes that's too many letters for even an eyeliner pencil to cope with, and because it can hardly be seen, let alone read, one or two letters often go missing, so that it reads 'Ad Onum Oms', or 'Ad Om Ons'. When this first happened last year, I felt like it was really naughty, and that the audience was bound to notice and letters would get sent, and we'd have to come up with some reason for the wrong spelling. 'I'm sorry everybody, Chris McCleod had his tattoo done while he was terribly drunk, as most soldiers are, and with a dyslexic tattooist.'

Oh dear, it looks like Billy Budd, the extra, has taken a real shine to Chris Gascoyne's friend Andy. The pair of them are inseparable. Actually, I think it's more a case of Billy not leaving Andy alone. Billy is the most extraordinary character. Last year for a bet, in the middle of a boiling hot July, he submerged his head in a huge bucket of slops after lunch. It was quite rancid as it had been standing in the hot sun for a good few hours, but this didn't deter Billy. It only made the dare more entertaining because no one thought he would actually go ahead and do it. But, of course, he did, and what was even worse was that there was a half-eaten sausage which he brought up between his teeth and proceeded to eat. Most of the spectators were too busy throwing up at this point

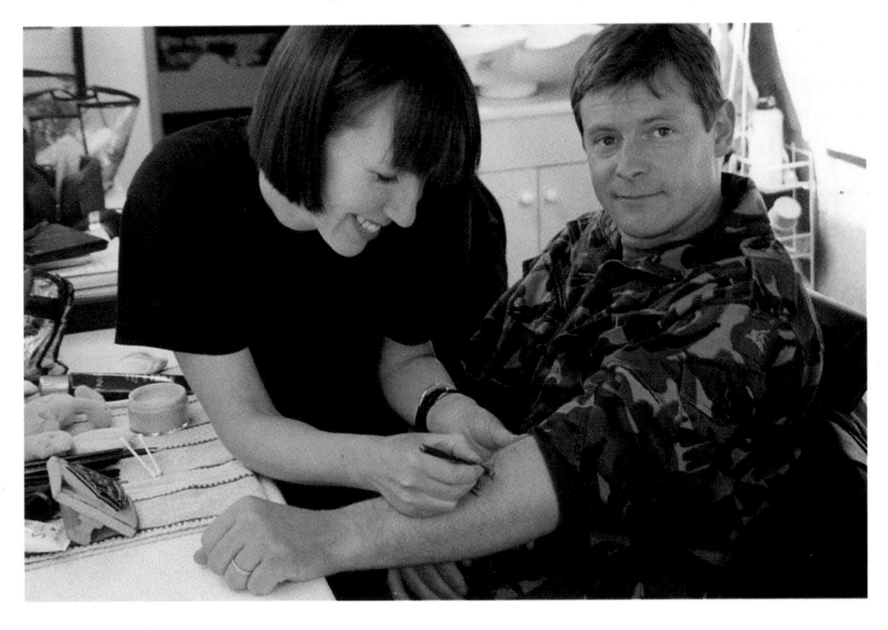

Left: If only I could have removed that beret – publicity still taken by Cliff Kent. Right: My tattoo is instantly applied with a stamp and then touched-up with an eye-liner pencil by Stella O'Farrell. This was a daily event taking about 20 minutes.

to part with the fifty quid which was the eventual total he managed to con out of the horrified crowd.

It was only then that I realised Billy was actually mad, and that this all stemmed from the fact that he'd been trained by the Royal Marines to kill people and got a terrifying buzz from pushing himself over the edge. The terrible irony, which he only revealed this year, was the fact that following his disgusting act of sheer debauchery, he developed a nagging ear infection which cost him a total of £55 in medication.

Suddenly told I can go home tonight. I'm not in the last scene of the day, and they're only prepared to put us up if there isn't a ten-hour break between the last scene today and first scene tomorrow.

Wednesday 4 June Episode 7

7.15am pick-up, not 5am as first feared. Turned out to be 7.30 as Ben was late. He'd turned the alarm clock off in his dream, or so he thought, until Rav was ringing on his doorbell. It's the first time I've known Ben to do this in two years. Chris Gascoyne and his friend Andy say they are going to stay at Hankley tonight, whatever, although as soon as we get there, Amanda (ideal casting: Glasgow Spice), who's the second AD that took over from Highland Spice a few days ago, says we are now all down here for the rest of the week and that is official.

My first scene today will be my last with Fiona in this series, as Fi is not coming out to Africa. Her character, Angela, is playing one of the 'civ pop' in the exercise. Lawrence, the love rival, is also involved in the exercise as some kind of medical intermediary, helping the 'civ pop' to find aid and bargaining with the King's Own. So, of course, he is all over Angela, which really winds up Chris. This particular scene is where the 'civ pop' have been allowed into the compound – code named 'Damascus' – which we have supposedly secured.

Andy Butcher (Danny Cunningham) is a casualty in the operation – after

Left: A very tragic civ pop (here featuring Jo, Pip and Fiona) – or The Killing Fields of Hankley.

triggering a mine to go off shortly after the road block incident – and is designated as having had his balls blown off. Danny can't, of course, refer to his balls as balls, because people don't do that on prime-time television. In the script, they were referred to as his 'tackle', which was OK, but Danny wanted to call them his 'plums', and that bearing in mind he'd just had his 'plums' blown off he wouldn't be able to get up off the stretcher and leave the shed as Chris asks him – so that Chris could be alone with Angela for a few minutes. But 'plums' was definitely out as far as the office was concerned.

Madeleine very diligently rang the office to run it by them, as we would be the ones who got it in the neck if one of us ever did say anything that was unscripted or not authorised by the office (God forbid that we should ever do such a thing)! So 'tackle' it was, but I liked 'tackle' all along, and I tried to convince Mr Cunningham of the benefits of 'tackle' over those of 'plums'. And although he took the 'tackle' decision on the chin, I think he'd become quite attached to 'plums' in his own quiet way.

To round off the scene, Chris and Angela then get their short piece of time alone together at which point Chris embarrasses himself by asking her if she has slept with the vet.

The scene was done in the one shot, there were to be no close-ups, no other set-ups. That was it. After the first take, though, Simon Okin, the sound recordist, wasn't happy, so he and his daughter, Delta (ideal casting: 'take those glasses off Miss Jones, you're beautiful') plastered the soles of our boots with black gaffer tape to try to muffle the heavy crunch of our footsteps in and out of the hut.

On the second take I slipped on the lino flooring with a heavy metal bucket full of hot water – narrowly avoiding tragedy.

On the third take, Chris King asked if I needed a stunt double to carry in the bucket of water. It looked so heavy he felt sorry for me, and he didn't want to feel sorry for me.

On the fourth take, bits of gaffer tape started peeling off my boots – felt like I was walking in chewing gum.

So suddenly we were up to five takes. Had visions of trying to eke out this scene for the rest of the day – it's only 11.30am, I don't think so. Marcia, the new first AD for this episode, throws in a few, 'Come on fellas, and knock it off, we're trying to work.' Ah! It's good to have Marcia back. Her familiar dulcet tones emanate over walkie talkies throughout the whole of Hankley Common. It hasn't been the same this year without her. Marcia firsted for nearly half of the entire series last year on every other episode.

After the fifth take, silence, then 'Cut! That's the one. Thank you everybody. Moving on.' Dermot, the focus puller, 'checks the gate', as it's called (see box, left) and everyone waits nervously. You can bet any money that if you've done an Oscar-winning performance in one take there will undoubtedly be a huge hair in the gate, and you'll have to go again. We get the 'Gate's clear' from Dermot, and then, 'Right, everyone's now officially on the wrong set,' booms Marcia down her walkie talkie.

Within seconds, the Nissan hut is cleared and empty apart from stretchers, the bucket and Fiona and me. We step out into glorious sunshine and I tell Fiona that this was

THE TECHNICALITIES:

Checking the gate

When the camera gate is being checked, it is to see if any hairs or bits of dust have somehow found their way into those vital areas of the equipment, because if they have they will scratch the negative, and you'll see a dirty great blob or hair in lots of frames. This, of course, makes it unusable.

our last scene together this year. She bursts out laughing.

FIONA	What is it you want me to do?
ME	I don't know. Maybe not look quite so happy.
FIONA	Is it a present you're after?
ME	No. Course not. Well, only a small one. It obviously hasn't hit you yet. The shock of it. You'll be an emotional mess next week. You mark my words.

2.30pm. 'Civ pop' had another afternoon off, as it was more driving. This is actually the first Land Rover driving I've done in two series, and I was starting to enjoy it.

3.30pm. Utterly bored of driving this dinosaur. I'm having to drive it up a steep hill with Ben (Captain Jeremy Forsythe) in the passenger seat, and Ian Driver (Captain Somers) sitting in the back, and I've got to hit a mark right at the top of a huge hill which overlooks the camp. Ben has to say in a very Glenn Ford sort of way, 'So there it is, Damascus.' But they keep changing the mark, bringing it as close to the edge as you possibly could go without it rolling down the other side of the hill and us with it. Ben offers a very cheery thought. 'Don't worry about us Jon, we'll be able to jump clear.'

I could see myself hurtling down the hill in a runaway Land Rover and being squashed as Ben and Ian are thrown clear. They finally turn the Land Rover upright, and the whole of my top half is in the shape of a steering wheel. I see the headline on 'News at Ten' with Trevor talking about 'the tragedy that befell the set of "Soldier, Soldier" today when one of their leading actors and brightest stars, if not their very brightest, well nearly as bright as the little one with the cute smile, was crushed to death after a stunt went horribly wrong. Exclusive pictures in part two.'

Why does my mind always go into over-activity and vivid detail of this sort of thing happening to me? Half joking, I make a thing about being insured. No one finds it funny. Worried whispering among the crew. All I catch is, 'No, it's all right. He can do it. Anyway, it's a full frontal of the both of them, so he's got to do it.' I guess that they're talking about the mark. No one wants to look me directly in the eye. All the crew start smiling and nodding at me, hoisting very positive thumbs-up signs to me.

Peter Greenhalgh, the director of photography, sticks a second camera right underneath me on the track that I would hurtle down if anything did go wrong, and I forgot a handbrake or that sort of thing. At least Peter has got confidence in me. I interpreted his gesture as very heroic, until I saw him look at where he'd put the camera tripod in relation to the brow of the hill, and then a look of 'you've got to be joking' came over his face as he hurriedly moved it all five yards over and up onto the safety of the mound above the track. Thought it best not to remind them of the incident way back in February with me, Queen Victoria, and a runaway BMW.

Genuinely felt frightened when it came to the take. Poor Ian. I reassured myself that accidents like that couldn't happen on 'Soldier, Soldier', it was all too professional. Then that horrible nagging little voice says, 'Always a first time!' Well, it came to it, and we got the 'action' from Marcia over a walkie talkie stuck to the inside of the dashboard, and I accelerated up the hill, having to keep two four-tonners, driven by Tom and Ian, right in my sights behind me, so that Martin could keep them in the frame. I got right to the very top,

bang on the mark, and stopped. It couldn't have been more perfect.

'Hold on fellas. We'll have to go again. Where were you four-tonners?' The four-tonners had big trouble getting up the hill and then Tom had big trouble getting the brake to work in time. When I look round after the 'cut', I was shocked to see Tom's grinning face, winking at me with the cab of his four-tonner kissing the rear bumper of our Land Rover.

The second take was even more perfect, even the driver from Action Vehicles gave me a nodding approval.

Back to the hotel for eight-ish. Andy's vibrating pager continues to go off occasionally, causing him great alarm as only his partner has the number. He, of course, assumes every time she rings that she has gone into labour. This time, however, it's the lottery results from earlier this evening. It's a free service with the pager.

We all had a meal together in the restaurant – bit of a 'heat the scampi up in the microwave' experience. Still, the Italian waiter was very

Above: Michelle Butterly can't decide which side she wants to be on. Right: Peter Greenhalgh, the DOP, with his camera carefully positioned in a damp area.

sweet. I think Michelle Butterly (Julie Oldroyd) wants to adopt him as her father. She certainly arranges a big enough tip for him to pay for arranging the adoption papers.

As well as Michelle, there's Jo (Karen Fitzpatrick), who I sit opposite, Fiona, who is next to me, Conor, Lee and Sarah (who play Conor's children, Kevin and Lucy Fitzpatrick), and Pip, who's here with his burgeoning wife and young daughter. I impress them all with my majestical Donald Duck impersonations. Pip's daughter thinks I am Walt Disney.

'Can you do the Lion King?'

How can anyone do the Lion King?

After dinner we sit in the 'lounge' whiling away the rest of the night. Fiona and Conor sing Celtic folk songs while the rest of us boring Anglos feel cheated of anything remotely folky to sing. In desperation, Michelle tries to get a round of 'Kumbayar' going. Not an especially good idea. So she goes off to borrow some cooking wine from the kitchen as we've now run out of anything to drink, and our good landlord has disappeared, locking everything in sight. Fiona moves on to renditions of proper songs and she can really sing them. I bet she used to practise for hours on end in front of the mirror in her bedroom with her hairbrush as her microphone. Got the sneakiest feeling she might still be at it. The rest of us now feel about as talented as rain in a puddle. We retire to our rooms.

Thursday 5 June Episode 7

Some kind of joke is definitely happening at my expense. For some unknown reason I am being brought in at 6.45am. Half an hour before any of the other boys and at the same time as Fiona and Jo. They're not even seeing my tattoo all week because my sleeves are down so it can't be because of that.

I deliberately oversleep, allowing a call from reception to tell me my Previa is waiting for me downstairs. It's now 7am. I feel this is the proper time I should have been called.

Not quite Bruce Willis, but it felt like a huge personal triumph of good sense as I waited 25 minutes before anyone wanted to see me in make-up.

Talk to members of the civ pop most of the day, as much of it is spent hanging around. Martin, the third AD, seems keen on one of them. It turns out they've been out together a couple of times. She's tall and gorgeous (ideal casting: Sandra Bullock). All the boys have clocked her and grumble over the fact that Martin got in there first – particularly Chris Gascoyne, who keeps sighing and shaking his head.

Then, news spreads like wild fire that her husband was in the SAS. Everyone immediately fears for Martin's health. Chris stops sighing and shaking

ABOVE: Chris Gascoyne playing at soldiers with Rob the armourer, the most lucrative job on the film set.
RIGHT: Boys with toys. Ben Nealon and me.
FAR RIGHT: Is this Hankley Common or Nam?

his head. Then the news changes. He's the ex-husband. You could see the faces all working away. 'I wonder if that means he's not as fit as he was.' 'I wonder what he's doing now!' 'God! I hope he hasn't become an assassin!'

Lots of bitty little scenes, and then the attack by Orange Forces which goes wrong because they use smoke without telling us. Still, managed to get nearly 500 rounds off, on automatic, at 39p a shot. Major Claude, the military advisor, is trying to find out why it is that the army get rounds at 9p and Carlton have to pay 39p.

At lunch time we had our injections for Africa: one in the bum and one in the arm. Only typhoid and hep A for me as I had some done a few years ago for a holiday in the Gambia.

I'm becoming obsessed with getting the best shots for this diary. The camera comes everywhere with me. It's a great little machine that's very forgiving, with a fantastic long zoom. I think the boys are getting a bit sick of me sneaking up on them and clicking away, though. I even took it the loos to try to get a few pictures of the 'honey wagon' and Conor, who was coming out of one of the cubicles and doing his trousers up, suddenly stared at me, horrified. I felt terribly embarrassed – as if I'd suddenly been caught with my pants down. I could see he instinctively wanted to grab the camera out of my hands and rip out the film, but his outward behaviour was very restrained. 'Is this for the diary, or for personal use?'

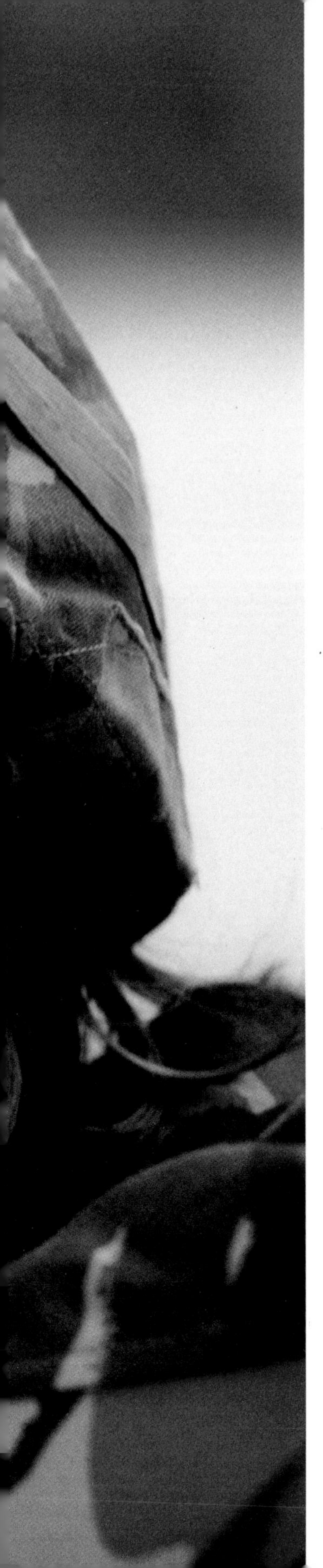

I tried, pathetically, to explain to him my running gag about the honey wagon, and wanting to get some photos of it so that the audience would have some visual reference. Conor just looked appalled. 'Jonathan! It's a toilet. And a toilet, is a toilet, is a toilet.'

He was right, of course. And it adds to my theory that the cast and crew might think the whole diary thing is a figment of my imagination. 'Yeah. Sure Jonathan. It's being published – right. Even the toilet bit!'

Found out that Conor's cousin is Larry Mullen of U2 fame. Now feel a complete berk, and presume Conor will, from now on, always see me as some kind of sad toilet trainspotter. As a result, I decide my best bet is to go into overkill with camera pointed at all sorts of other ridiculous aspects of life on a film set – purely for Conor's benefit, in the hope that he thinks I'm sad, but eccentric and interesting, as opposed to just sad. Photos of spent shell cases which have been wedged into polystyrene coffee cups in pretty patterns, close-ups of doughnuts, that sort of thing.

In the evening, we all go into Guildford for a night out. This is the first time we've done it as a big group. Shaun Matthew arranges the free entry at the club, and we have a fun night dancing and drinking.

The highlight happened on our return to our hotel, The Pride of the Valley. During the course of the week, Billy Budd was continuously all over Andy, the extra. At one point I even turned round and managed to catch Billy giving Andy an Eskimo kiss – yes, they were rubbing noses. No, that's not totally accurate, actually Billy was holding the back of Andy's head while he rubbed his nose against Andy's grimacing face. Andy was actually quite worried about Billy's attentions and confided his concerns to Chris, who he had come with to the set in the first place. 'Was Billy gay? Is that what it was all about?' Chris played along and very convincingly assured him that although Billy quite likely fancied

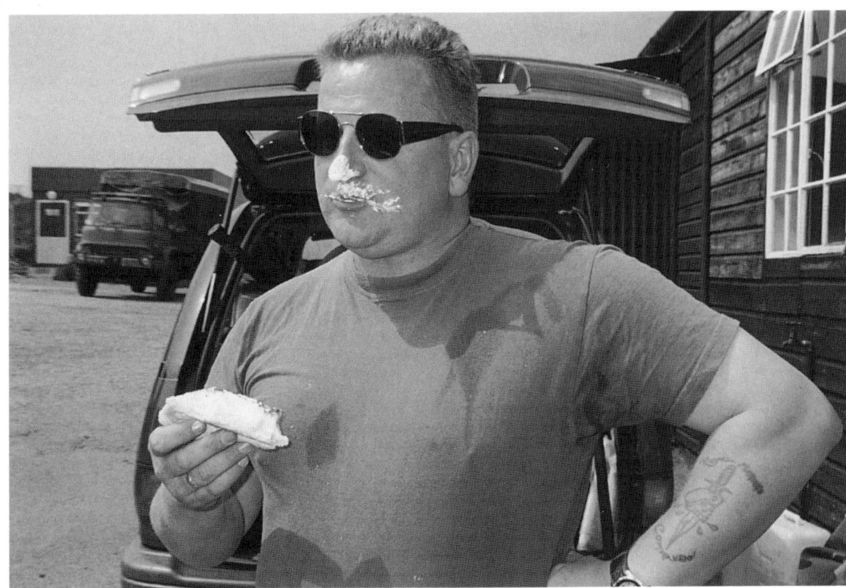

Left: Sarah Smart, who plays Alan Fitzpatrick's daughter Lucy, ready to 'go, go, go.'
Above: Billy Budd. His coordination has never been the same since he left the Royal Marines.

Andy, he probably wouldn't do anything about it.

'Probably?!', replied Andy, 'What do you mean probably?' That evening in the club, Andy stuck to Chris like a limpet, and every time he looked over at Billy, he was looking back, and on one occasion even blew Andy a kiss. We were all in on the joke and it was hard to keep it going for as long as we did.

When we got back to The Pride of the Valley we all said goodnight and went upstairs to our rooms. What happened next was reported to me. Apparently, Andy had gone into the bedroom he was sharing with Chris. He put the door on the latch and sat on the edge of his bed, and took his contact lenses out while he waited for Chris to come upstairs. As the door opened, he did an enormous double take, because standing in front of him wasn't Chris. Andy got a terrible shock and leapt over the bed. It was Billy standing there, totally naked, singing 'My Little Buttercup'.

This went on for several minutes with Andy pleading to Billy, even grabbing a beer bottle to defend himself, while outside everyone else was in tears of laughter, and Andy was telling Billy it wasn't funny any more.

Friday 6 June Episode 7

Picked-up again at 6.45am. What is going on? The location is five minutes away. Again, waited till 7am and then when I got to the set had to wait until 7.30am before anyone wanted me in make-up. These long waits only encourage me to eat more breakfast. I always start with the good intention course – a nice healthy bowl of grapefruit segments or prunes or both mixed together into a very exotic sweet and sour taste bud tickler, which never fails to lure me into a smug sense of achievement.

Five minutes later, I can be found hovering round the croissants – just one – with two little squares of butter, because they're very fattening. That always goes down with a very moreish follow through, so I make my first appearance in the queue for something hot – a bowl of porridge. Brown sugar obviously, because refined sugar's so bad for you.

Then it's a quick head round the door of the make-up wagon to check it's still the girls being seen to, before getting back in that queue for a crack at the main event – the fry-up. Alison comes over to hustle me back to the make-up wagon. Little does she realise, I nipped in when I did. Always try to leave a second AD stumped for what to say. By the time they've checked out your story, the chances are they've dealt with three phone calls and a lot extra, and will have forgotten all about you. You then just have long enough to take your fry-up and hide on the eating coach, before they remember and know exactly where to find you. The only crucial decision is whether to be boringly righteous and ask the cook to make you a couple of poached eggs – which can, on the negative side, cut down on your eating time as they have to be specially made – or do you plump for the cholesterol gobbet of fried eggs.

Today, Chris King wanted to do the impossible – a four page dialogue scene, involving all the main principles who had been down on Hankley Common this week, in one shot. ONE SHOT! He didn't want the camera to stop moving. He wanted a continuous flow from one huddle of characters talking, to the next, and so on, and the camera which was mounted on a crane would come in and out and up and down throughout the five minute scene. Ambitious was not the word.

We are talking 'ER' time. He gathered us all round him and we read the lines before he told us what he wanted to happen. Then we plotted it out very roughly. Chris McCleod walks from Kevin Fitzpatrick (son of Alan), who is lying unconscious on the ground after being knocked down by a Land Rover, taking the camera with him to Andy Butcher and Jacko Barton. They have a little exchange before Chris leaves, again taking the camera with him but as he walks into another discussion with one of the Orange Forces soldiers the camera stays on Angela McCleod, Julie Oldroyd and Tony Rossi.

The camera then follows Corporal Mark Hobbs as he comes over to this group and starts having a go at the Orange Forces soldier, blaming him for the accident as they had used smoke grenades, which hadn't been planned. The camera then pans to Lt Colonel Drysdale's Land Rover as it enters the compound. Alan Fitzpatrick jumps out to look at his son, who is still lying on the ground, and then the camera leaves Fitzpatrick to go to Drysdale who starts giving Fitzpatrick a bollocking for allowing the boy to be run over in the first place.

The climax of the scene involves Hobbs shouting at Drysdale and accusing him of not taking responsibility and being a bully. Chris McCleod pulls him away, but it's too late by then. He has already done enough to destroy whatever future he had in the army. In a way, Hobbs is saying all the things everyone else has only had the courage to think, which is why Chris doesn't pull him away sooner. The final moments of the scene are of everyone watching Hobbs as he leaves the compound, taking off his uniform as he goes.

This was going to be a huge undertaking to do in one shot. There were so many technical things to get right such as marks for the dolly, which the grip had to be responsible for, and keeping the focus sharp as the camera moved in and out. And there were fifty or sixty extras who all had to be involved and listening. If one of them was grinning or not really with it, it could ruin the entire shot. It was one of the few times when everyone had a chance to show exactly how good they were. And it was particularly thrilling for the actors, as it meant we all had to know exactly who said what and when. It was almost like being on stage.

There were strict marks we all had to hit, but without there being any sausages or gaffer tape on the marks as the entire ground of the compound was going to be in shot at one time or another. I thought we would be there all day. This sort of shot is so rarely attempted that I assumed it would take a while for everyone to warm up and begin to work as a team. This is what they do on 'NYPD Blue' or 'ER', and here we were trying to go for something as interesting as that. This would certainly be a day to remember.

We did a similarly exhilarating take this time last year, in the war episode. A group of us walked towards a waiting helicopter with blades whizzing round just above our

BEHIND-THE-SCENES:

The caterers

The caterers have the hardest job on the entire film set. They have to start preparing breakfast at 5.30am. Then they are on the go the whole day, clearing away, serving, preparing the meal, buying the food, and making sure there's tea and coffee and snacks and fruit constantly available. And this is for at least a hundred people, from the back of a mobile kitchen, often in a field in the middle of nowhere.

They often will have made the lunch for a certain time, and then are told half an hour before they are due to serve it that lunch is being delayed until a particular shot or set-up has been finished on the set. So patience is incredibly important. It must be terribly frustrating if you have created something delicious in such cramped conditions for such a lot of people, only to be told, 'Oh by the way, you'll have to keep it warm for the next hour.'

The guys from Set Meals are used to this, of course, as this is one of the pitfalls of working as a caterer on a film set. But they assure me that there are many plusses – although none of them could think of very many when I talked to them.

heads and climbed in it. It was done with a Steadicam on top of a crane which lowered as we walked out of the compound, and the Steadicam operator then stepped off the crane and carried on walking alongside us to the helicopter. Coincidentally, that scene was also shot at this same location. On the same afternoon, we also did the 200 metre running Steadicam shot of us leaving the crashed helicopter and dashing into the woods to find safety.

Today, after several rehearsals we were actually ready to shoot a take. Everyone was getting nervous. I hadn't seen anything like this all year.

Chris King did something crucial at this point. He came out from behind his monitor, and he told all of us – crew, actors, extras, everyone – how important every individual contribution would be to make this a success. And he also added that if it was going to work at all, it was likely to be in the first three or four takes. We all felt the temperature rise by several degrees.

The first take stumbled to a halt two-thirds of the way through. It had been going so well, but suddenly it seemed to crumble. I think Ian (Corporal Hobbs) was feeling the strain as it was his emotional blow-out that was crucial for the end to have the impact that Chris King was after. It tends to happen like that. You'll rehearse the shot to a point where you think you're ready to shoot it, but then when it comes to the take, someone or everyone suddenly forgets lines that they knew perfectly well in every single rehearsal.

ABOVE: Filming from on high. Dermot the focus puller is wondering if he can fit in a quick bungee jump before the take.

Sometimes I think the director should be really sneaky and not tell the actors that they're going for a take, as I think the sheer fact that the actor is suddenly aware that there is film in the camera and it is rolling can throw the actor into a bit of a spin. It can have the opposite effect on other actors, though. Peter Sellers, for example, was renowned for getting the shot in the first take and he hated to do more than a couple of takes, whereas Terry Thomas, would often need hundreds of takes before he got the one the director was happy with. I think the most I've ever needed on Soldier was nine or ten. I'm sure if you made a habit of needing double figures, the old P45 would be waiting in the caravan after a few days.

The second take was OK, but a bit tentative, and Chris King said as much. I started dwelling on what he'd said about doing it in three or four takes. Was it going to be this one? Ian sat psyching himself up, last minute alterations and tweaks went on, a light was moved. We then waited for what seemed like an age for the sun, which went behind a very big cloud. Could we keep the concentration? Who was going to be the next one to forget a line or jump in too early?

The third take was good. I thought we had it. The crew clapped. But

Chris wanted just one more. How could he? So we went again straight away. The adrenaline was still pumping, the sun was still out. The fourth take really was the one. It had energy, it seemed technically on the nail and Chris was happy. The crew clapped again. I 'deja vued' we were in Hollywood. We all had a great patting ourselves on the back session. 'I thought you were excellent.' 'And it could only have been as good as that because you were so "there".'

Chris was genuinely thrilled with what we'd done. He came forward after it was all over and the tension was dissipating into relief, and he announced that in all his twenty years of directing in television, this had been the most exciting shot he'd managed to achieve. And I think we all believed him. He also admitted that he hadn't been at all sure it was going to work – although you would never have known that from the first rehearsals of the scene only four hours earlier.

The incredible thing was that we did a four-minute shot and completed the whole thing before lunch. If we'd been able to do another scene like that in the afternoon, the resulting eight minutes would have been quite something, as this quantity of footage is unheard of. However, in the afternoon, we had to re-shoot part of a scene from Tuesday at the road block.

We tried to do the shot last thing yesterday, but the heavens opened just as we got to the location, and it was already 6pm. It was obvious that God was saying, 'That's a wrap boys, so don't push it.' When we finally did it late this afternoon, it was a real palaver trying to sort out who was where, and which hand had the rifle, and which had the log. This is where Madeleine and her little Polaroids came into their own (see box, below).

Saturday 7 June Episode 7

Last filming day in UK. 6.45am pick-up, yet again.

Only the one scene for me, so I should be through by lunch time. Working overtime with camera – mostly rubbish. Had my farewell doughnut. Wonder if they'll have doughnuts in Africa. Should I take my own? Perhaps I'll take photo of one to carry round with me. Maybe even take photo of me biting into one – no, too masochistic.

Discover Chris Gascoyne does very good impression of me. When I ask him to show me, he goes very sheepish and insists he can only do it with the gloves on. I go off in search of gloves. 'Why gloves?', I ask. 'It's just the way you use them. Hitting one hand against the other.' 'Didn't realise my glove acting had been such a hit.'

Chris also does other impressions. I ask him for his Daniel Day-Lewis from 'My Left Foot'. It's quite brilliant. The head twitches and the desperate attempt to speak out of the side of the mouth – if you close your eyes you can actually hear Daniel Day-Lewis saying 'Foch ploootonic!' Chris then goes on to imitate David Thewlis in a clip from the recent film 'The Island of Dr Moreau'. There is wonderful incongruity of his Yorkshire accent adrift in the Indian Ocean in a Hollywood movie alongside the likes of Marlon Brando.

THE TECHNICALITIES:

Continuity

If Madeleine hadn't meticulously gone round Polaroiding everything and writing it all down, there would have been no point us trying to do the re-shoot. It's amazing how quickly the brain discards information like, 'Where do I put my hat in this scene?', and, 'What do you mean I put my hand down from the windscreen on Captain Somers' line, "No Engineers!"? Was it my left or right hand?' That was ancient history as far as I was concerned. Today's another day for my grey matter.

LEFT: Meet the Ogdens: Danny Cunningham with his brother Peter who was an extra on the show for a week.

Nothing much to do this morning. There is a very long shot of us letting the 'civ pop' into the compound which is being filmed from way off on top of a hill – lots of opportunity for being silly, so must be careful. I get Peter, Danny's brother, to come with me and pour hot water into a bucket. I try to tell him as he acts his little cotton socks off that we're unlikely to be more than pin pricks on the screen, but there is no telling Pete. He's off. This is the movies. If I want water in a bucket he's going to give me the best water in a bucket you will ever have seen.

Finished just before lunch. That is it for me till Zim. Suddenly, it all seems to have gone too fast. Chris King has arranged a few beers over lunch. It's his last day too. Very nice gesture. He says a few words about how much he's enjoyed working with us. It's Ian's last day as well but he seems far less affected by it than me. I take my uniform off for the last time. The combat gear we wear in Africa will be different, so that is the last time I wear my combat jacket. Part of me wants to take them with me, but reality tells me different. When would I ever wear combat gear at home? I have a sudden vision of me doing the gardening in my uniform and my green wellies. No I don't think so. And I think M is thoroughly bored of anything military – I've been in it, written plays about it, acted in a series as a soldier. I think it's time to find something different. Perhaps I'll try to nick my beret for posterity when we finish in Zim.

Real sense of anticlimax when I get in the Previa for the last time. Rav is taking Chris, his friend Andy and me back to London. Still no news on Andy's imminent baby.

M is out with Abe when I get back, so sit down and write this. Then pace up and down the garden, looking at the shed and admiring the beautiful garden which M has created in less than six months. The roses are blooming, so are the lilies; and the clematis, which started out about six inches high, has grown rampantly all the way up the trellis. I must put another piece of trellis above the door for it to climb across.

An interlude

Saturday 14 June

Stills photo shoot at Sandhurst for publicity department. Tracey has organised the whole thing with Major Claude Davidson and apparently we are guests of the Gurkhas.

Picked up at 8.30am. They've allowed two hours for us to get there, and seeing as we're not even picking up Gascoyne, as he stayed over at the hotel last night with Tom in Reading, two hours seems ridiculous. Ben, John the driver (from 'Braveheart') and I stop for coffee and croissants, only I have one of the largest Danish pastries I have ever encountered. I make a solid effort up the pastry's north face, reaching the peak nearly half an hour later. I know the descent is going to be hell.

It's a lovely sunny morning and we sit outside at a small table contemplating the ludicrousness of allowing two hours for a journey that should take at the most forty minutes. Then we see Jane the 'Soldier, Soldier' nurse strolling along the pavement. Her eyes nearly pop out of their sockets. It's very odd suddenly seeing people you associate with your job in one location appearing in a completely different one and in a different context.

Jane was just popping out to the deli-come-patisserie for her morning bread, and the last thing she expected to see was familiar faces from the work groove. This was her day off. She immediately got a terrible fright and thought that the whole crew was around and that we were filming there and no one had told her. It was only after a few minutes of winding her up that she realised and asked us properly what we were doing there.

Sandhurst on a weekend is a hive of activity. It's like a cross between a big old boarding school, a university, and an open prison. This weekend was visiting time. All the cadets were dressed up in best bib and tucker, and there were displays being organised when we arrived. Lots of officers wandering around, presumably instructors with their dogs, either labradors, spaniels or Jack russells and all with names like 'Chaka' and 'Vivy', and looking terribly important – with swagger sticks or riding crops, and funny maroon-coloured trousers.

We've been allocated a big conference room in New College to get changed in and have make-up done. Someone's forgotten to pack the tattoo, so if we have any shots without jackets there will be a lot of me with my arms folded, or with my left arm cleverly hidden behind someone else's back.

I have a terrible urge to go out and walk around the parade ground, not dressed in the uniform properly, with hands in pockets and beret turned round the other way on the head like a cap, just to see if some grumpy old CSM or, even better, RSM, comes up and tries to get all hysterical with me. Hasn't happened to me yet sadly. It's not for want of trying. I got half dressed and walked out and about in front of New College, just daring for someone to come up and

take me to task, I would have thought if it doesn't happen here, it's not going to happen anywhere.

Tom, Chris, Ian and Danny all came out as well. Tom was still drinking his McDonald's cup of tea, Chris was smoking and had his T-shirt sleeves folded up on to his shoulders in his now familiar Vietnam at rest pose, and Ian and Danny were both 'shaded up' – definitely not regulation issue army sunglasses that's for sure. We all had that look of 'Come on then – where are you? Tell me off. Shout at me so I can shout back.' Pathetic. I think the real soldiers – the senior NCOs anyway – must have a sixth sense as they have always kept a very wide berth. Maybe they realised that a spectacle such as us looking the way we did was just too unbelievable to take even the slightest bit seriously.

The pictures were a laugh. Quite literally. It was hopeless. Never try to take serious photographs of a group of adults dressed up as soldiers, and expect them to take it seriously. It was impossible. The poor photographer was getting more and more frustrated, and at the same time trying to keep his cool, because he knew it wouldn't help if he blew a fuse as well. God knows, that might have been the final clincher that sent us into hysterical giggling. Here we were, dressed up in all the gear, packing all the guns and generally re-enacting most eleven year old boys' fantasies. This was 'Apocalypse Now', 'The Longest Day' and 'Full Metal Jacket' all rolled into one.

Loads of pouting, cocked eyebrows, and very little mascara – waterproof, of course. We even had smoke and explosions going off behind us as the camera clicked away. Having been told to expect a little bang behind us, it did come as quite a shock when a huge, thunderous, ground-shaking explosion rocked us off our feet. I'd love to see those pictures. I bet we looked about as tough as Julian Clary posing for *Soap Weekly*. We had individual poses shot as well, which is another killer when you are standing in front of your peers. I think that individual photo sessions are on a par with the dentist. They should be one on one behind closed doors – with something to catch the spit. If you asked most actors, I'm sure they'd say that they hate having them done.

Chris looks so uncomfortable, it's painful to watch, and it's only when he decides to take off his helmet and have some done '*sans* bucket' that he stops looking like Bill and Ben, one of the Flowerpot Men. But talking of Ben, the other Ben, Ben Nealon – the old master – he's a lesson to watch. Concentrated, ignoring the crowd, just loving the camera and letting the camera love him.

Lunch with the Gurkhas. And what a spread they put on. It was pristine white tablecloths on tables outside their bar with lots of regimental silverware proudly displayed. The senior Gurkha officers had turned out specially. The trouble is it's very hard to take their angelic, warm-hearted faces seriously. I mean when you think about it, these boys are some of the most deadly warriors in the world – infamous for their close-quarter fighting and those scythe like knives which they use to cut off heads and disembowel sheep. And here they are beaming and nodding away. Nothing is too much trouble.

The Gurkha curry they made for us, with all the chutneys, rice and pickles, was absolutely exquisite. It was so delicious I felt I should aim for seconds and thirds, although I needn't have worried about appearing greedy. They kept producing more and more of the stuff, so it was no good sitting there making all

LEFT: The King's Own mean business. A publicity still from the Sandhurst shoot taken on 14 June – or is it a deodorant advert?

the right noises, cleaning your plate and waiting for the pud, because they were up like a flash, soon as your cutlery had hit the table, putting plate to serving dish and ladling out more.

Above: Lunch, as served by the Gurkhas at the Royal Military Academy, Sandhurst.

I sat chatting over my lunch to two Gurkhas, one in his late thirties and about to leave the regiment, and therefore securing that most prized of possessions, his pension, and a younger Gurkha who was in his late twenties. You could see his eyes light up every time the word pension was mentioned. They only get paid leave once every three years, and none of them can really afford to pay for a leave all the way back home – they send most of their wages back in the first place to support their families. It's a six month long leave and they go home, make their wives pregnant, hang out for a few more months and then don't see the child they have helped to create for the next two-and-a-half years. I can't even imagine what it would be like not to see Abraham until he's two-and-a-half. If you talk to any Gurkha you soon find out they all have children with two-and-a-half year gaps between them. And the soldiers and their partners put up with this situation for years and years and years.

The final set of photos takes place with us up to our knees in water. A spot was found that looked straight out of a World War Two Burmese jungle. We look like we're doing the publicity stills for a production of 'The Long and the Short and the Tall'. Tom keeps trying to pull Chris's sleeves down, but I think Chris has finally warmed up and he's starting to enjoy it – he's found his angle. He's hiding behind his tattoos. Chris has a pair of incredibly impressive tattoos.

One at the top of each shoulder. They make my winged Pegasus look quite limp and restrained, and remind me that I haven't got it on in the first place. Let's hope it isn't noticeable.

At the end of the day, Tracey and John the photographer seemed pleased. Tracey also gave me a copy of all the contact sheets containing every photo taken on 'Soldier, Soldier' this year so far. There must be nearly a thousand photos to look at.

Tuesday 17 June

Met Sian Facer in her office this morning. She showed me the dust jacket for the book. Had a sudden 'St Paul on the road to Damascus' vision that this was actually happening, and that there were other people busying themselves with the whole thing. She also enthusiastically showed me the inside cover of one of the book trade's recent publications showing a picture of the same dust jacket among other forthcoming autumn publications to look out for. Suddenly felt that a Kurdish goat herder's diary would be more interesting than my ramblings. Help. Feeling very insecure. Overwhelmed with the urge to give Sian a huge dose of me seeming confident. Don't think it worked. She kept talking to me like she was talking down a jumper from a roof.

Sian and I drove out from London to the set – the location is a regular one used by the series this year and it's near Bracknell. We went to meet Marilyn Moorhouse from Random House, the publisher (ideal casting: Prunella Scales), and various members of the book trade who are going to be selling the book when it comes out.

It was supposed to be a chance for them to see what really goes on when we're filming – a chance to watch a scene being rehearsed and shot, meeting the actors and director and having lunch with me. Unfortunately for them, it was up to me to be Mr Charming and show them round. When I introduced them to the boys, I could see lots of brains clicking over, wondering what incriminating evidence they'd blabbed to me. I think Chris, Tom, Conor and Ben had all thought this diary was a figment of my imagination. So suddenly meeting real people from the publishing world and seeing the dust jacket, which was closely scrutinised by one and all with nodding heads and 'why am I not on it?' smiles, was rather amusing.

CHRIS You won't actually print all the...you know...?
ME All the what, Chris?
CHRIS All the... you know.
TOM The embarrassing bits.
CHRIS Oooooo dear. You're not are you?
ME Course not.
CHRIS Because no one would be interested in any of that, would they?
ME No. No. Course not.
(Silence)
CHRIS Cup of tea, Jon?
ME Yeah. Lovely. Milk no sugar.
TOM It's all right. I'll get it.
CHRIS No. You're all right. I'm up now. Sticky bun while I'm there, Jon?

The visitors all seemed to have a suitably good time, although one of them, Jim, was sadly let down on one account. He'd been looking forward to seeing and holding one of the weapons – the SA 80 rifle, but unfortunately none of the scenes today involved any firing. So the best we could come up with was one of our plastic alternatives which look just like the real thing but half the weight (see box, below).

Before I left, I went onto the wardrobe bus, and picked out a few items from Chris McCleod's wardrobe that I thought would also look good in Jonathan Guy Lewis's wardrobe, gave Andy a cheque and said my goodbyes. Again. I probably wouldn't see most of the crew again until Africa.

THE TECHNICALITIES:

Stand-by props

Nick (ideal casting: the voice of Tommy Cooper and the body of an overweight cherub) does the 'Soldier, Soldier' stand-by props and he looks after and hands out all those props that are needed in the scene being filmed at any particular time. We use lightweight substitutes nearly all the time as they are far more practical for filming purposes. There are only ten of the real ones available for blank firing – so the choreography of who has which rifle in which shot depends very much on who the camera is favouring each time. If it's a close-up on a couple of you, then of course, you both get the real guns to fire. But if there's a large fire fight like there was at Hankley Common a couple of weeks ago, involving more than ten of the cast, it has to be carefully stage-managed for the camera as to who has the real firing ones. On the screen, of course, it looks like we're all blasting away with the real thing – but, hey, isn't that just the magic of TV?!

ABOVE: Look who's grabbed the biggest gun!
RIGHT: By the left – Danny Cunningham and Tom Craig share a joke at Chris Gascoyne's expense – he just couldn't get into the picture in time.

Tuesday 24 June

6am phone call from a James Christopher in Mutare wanting to introduce himself and touch base. 'James Christopher what?' M says. 'I'll touch his base all right. What's he doing calling at 6 o'clock in the morning?' 'Was the last bit cut off?', I ask myself. Is he Jimmy Chrissy to his friends? Does he have friends when he calls people at 6 o'clock in the morning? It transpires that he's the second assistant director for Africa. The ansaphone takes the call. M does her early morning Charles Manson impression. I'm now fearful for Jamie Christopher's safety should they ever meet. He says he's going to phone back later. Does that mean two in the morning?

Busy in the British Library Reading Room as it's too damp in the shed. Rain. Rain. Rain. Rain. Rain. You have to get to the Reading Room early or it's impossible to find one of the special workplaces where you can plug into a socket for the old laptop. But I miss my view of the garden in all its glory, and being able to see into all the various flats, not only in our big old house, but next door on both sides. When I'm in the shed after dark and all the lights are on and our various neighbours' lives are going on – TVs blaring, arguments, lights flickering – it looks just like a scene out of Hitchcock's 'Rear Window', where James Stewart is wheelchair-bound and witnesses a neighbour murdering his wife. Not that I'm suggesting anything as extreme as that is going on, but it does bring out the curious in me. M says voyeur.

I'm now in the middle of a major headache – how to make sense and order of a large bundle of disparate pieces of paper with diary entries written all over the place. There are entries written on different scripts, pink pages, blue pages, schedules. So at least my section of the 'Soldier, Soldier' rainforest is getting some recycling.

Meeting Ian (Curtis) at 11am in Soho to look through his photos to see if there are any we can use for the diary. My voice-over agent is putting me up to do the voices in a recently animated cartoon, so I've got to drop in a tape to her on the way of another cartoon series which I did voices for a few years ago called 'Juniper Jungle'. From the sublime to the ridiculous. A soldier, hero and TV actor to 'Jock the Croc' in one fell swoop. Still you take what you can get 'guvnor' when you've got a child to support.

Suddenly my meeting with Ian in Café Bohem turns into a 'Soldier, Soldier' reunion. Danny and Chris appear from nowhere with Shaun Matthew who had driven them to an ADR session, but it was running over so they had come to Café Bohem for a drink while they waited. Then up popped Tom who'd come in for a quiet drink with a friend. He initially looked quite hurt, thinking we'd arranged it all and hadn't included him. We had to work hard to convince him that it was complete coincidence.

3.15pm ADR session for episode 8 – also in Soho, thank God. It's the rugby and it's one line. The director and sound technician want a more definite reading of the line which, as I explain to them, was meant to be a sarcastic aside and not a big public utterance to all the other players on my side which was what my next line was. However, they remain unconvinced so I give them a couple of interpretations for Crispin to listen to, although I'm still sure that the original was far better. 'But who am I to reason why? I'm just there to ADR, then 'bye'.

The rugby itself looks good, but the sequences are over in a flash, and you think, did it really take all day to just do those bits? Those Reading boys seem even bigger on film, which makes us 'Soldier, Soldier' boys stick out even more – we could be mistaken for spare pork sausages at a bar mitzvah. Still be positive. There have to be short ones. There always have to be short ones. Not everyone can be the size of Ben Clarke.

Abraham said 'Oh shit' this evening while eating dinner. This is the first time he's said anything like that, and he must have deduced from mine and Miranda's reaction that he was on to a real winner. I was finding it very hard not to laugh, while M was open mouthed, and insistent with both me and Abe that it wasn't funny – which, of course, it was. The more he said it, the more I laughed. Eventually M cracked as well, and we all had a lovely family supper and bath time while Abe entertained us with his 'Oh shit' and farting in the bath.

Friday 27 June

10.30 am meeting with Penny Simpson (ideal casting: Imogen Stubbs) at the publishers, to go through photos. I arrive – bag nervous, heart heavy. No. Wrong way round. Bag heavy, heart nervous. Actually heart loud. Decide best tactic is to bury Penny in sea of photos and contact sheets. Tactic works. Out at 1pm.

Miranda has recall for a film this afternoon. Recall to do a reading of a film. What is going on? Next they'll be expecting us to audition for an audition. There's no money involved, only expenses. It's always the same – three auditions, a recall and a tortuous Saturday afternoon workshop to do an acting job at a fringe theatre in Shepherd's Bush. If you're lucky, you might get your bus pass paid. But then one interview filmed on video and sent out to Hollywood could get you a part in a movie, or sent off to some advertising agency could earn you thousands for a few days' work on a commercial.

Back in the shed all afternoon. Why is it I can't sit on my orthopaedically responsible seat for more than half-an-hour without it hurting my whole body? It's one of those ones that you kneel on and it supports your lower back and knees. I seem to be finding every excuse possible this afternoon to stop myself from sitting down and writing. Even contemplated cutting the grass. Went back into the garden, walked up and down the lawn admiring all the flowers. Put some military marching band music on to try to put me in the mood. I often find that listening to music while I write can unlock the inspiration. This is the Marching Band of the Royal Air Force, playing movie theme classics.

The next thing I remember was Miranda and Abraham knocking on one of the windows, and me waking with a start. I had apparently slept for a good forty minutes, with my head on my hands on the table, and I'd dribbled all down the side of my face.

Monday 30 June

Spent all weekend in mad scramble to decipher the rest of my notes. Hard to keep track of which episode was filmed when as not one episode was shot in order, so can't track it back logically. First was episode 3 then episode 2 then episode 4, then 1, 6, 5, and so on. Keep drifting off into reminiscences of last year's series and this one. All things considered, this really has been one hell of a job. And the icing on the cake is just about to come.

I'm going to Africa – today. Africa. I still have to keep telling myself it's true. I've got a little world atlas in the shed and I keep glancing over to it. There's England up here, and down there is Africa. AFRICA. I'm being paid to work in AFRICA. Elation is quickly swept away, however, as I glance over to the picture of Abraham and Miranda on the other side of my table. It means nearly four weeks without seeing them.

Phone call from the office. Apparently, a whole day's worth of filming has been damaged in the laboratory, and will have to be re-shot. This is a disaster for the schedule as it is tight enough as it is. The plan was for episode 12 to finish on the Friday and for most of the actors to fly out on Saturday on the night flight. The revised schedule now means redoing all the stuff that was lost on the Saturday during the day, and then flying that night.

Packing is last minute as usual and I'm only just ready in time when the taxi arrives at 4pm to take me to the airport. Alex Norton (ideal casting: a Glaswegian Raul Julia, or Alexei Sayle), who's playing Walker, the head of the Mercenary Force that Hobbs has joined, is also waiting in the taxi. Hate saying goodbyes so being distracted by diary and packing stops me from getting all emotional.

I'm in the taxi and away before my brain catches up with me and joins my body in the present. Meet up with Ian Curtis at the airport. Flying Air Zimbabwe. We take off at 9 o'clock, and the first thing the senior cabin steward says is, 'Our flight time is ten hours.' There's no one next to me, so I really can stretch out. The cabin staff are lovely, and nothing is too much trouble. Glass of bubbly before we take off. I knock it back, with disastrous consequences. My body just isn't made to consume alcohol at high altitude. One unit of alcohol at altitude for me translates to not just drunk, or even slurred-speech drunk, but falling-over drunk.

As soon as I manage to work out how the tray slides out of the arm rest I knock over all my peanuts and my secret Canadian Club – that I'm not even going to tell myself that I had – with the compact TV screen that slides out on an arm from the other rest. Everything ends up all over my nice clean trousers and the seat. I interpret this as the Maradona hand of God stepping in and saying, 'Oi, Lewis, NO. You can't hide the Canadian Club from me.' Just to keep me penitent, I'm left with a very pungent stale-whiskey-on-a-seat smell that wafts over the whole of the cabin.

I finally get to see Mike Leigh's film 'Secrets and Lies'. What a wonderful film. I watch it again straight after. Kate O'Malley (ideal casting: Juliette Binoche in 'The English Patient' or 'The Unbearable Lightness of Being Brummy') who plays the part of Private Stacey Butcher in 'Soldier, Soldier', spent six months working on the film. But, as is quite common with Mike Leigh's work, whole strands and story lines end up on the cutting room floor. So it was, sadly, with her story line. As an actor I can think of nothing more depressing than spending all that time working and improvising away, only to have your efforts completely lost. Not seen by anyone. I look out for her name

BEHIND-THE-SCENES

White hunter black heart

Alex Norton has been to Zimbabwe before. He was in a film called 'White Hunter, Black Heart' (nicknamed 'Dirty Harare'), directed by and starring Clint Eastwood. He tells me that he didn't meet Clint for either an audition or an interview, Clint was simply sent a video of Alex and decided to hire him from that. This proves another of my theories about this business. If Clint had been directing a profit-share theatre production at a fringe theatre, Alex would have had recall after recall, and then have had to pay for the privilege of working.

So when on the first morning of filming Clint walks past Alex, and actually says 'Morning Alex', Alex is understandably chuffed and surprised. 'Morning Clint.' Good title for Alex's autobiography: Clint Eastwood Knew my Name. Can't believe we are now working with an actor who is – or has been – on first name terms with Clint Eastwood.

RIGHT: Alex Norton (Colonel Walker), in his 'I love it when you're strict' pose

on the credits and at least it's there.

I haven't seen anything of the lovely Kate so far this year, but she's coming out to Africa, and I've even got a little scene with her. I'm sure we'll do lots of catching up at the hotel. The seats aren't really comfortable enough to sleep in, and I keep seeing a vision of Helen Mirren's legs stretching out on the Virgin advert, and her telling me to concentrate on the room in front.

We land in Harare at 7am, although they are an hour ahead of the UK here, so that makes it 8am. It's been a pretty uncomfortable time, but we've arrived. Africa. The equator. 'More sun in their winter than our summer' Africa. The first thing I'd noticed in the night sky or early morning sky as we crossed the equator was the moon. It was a crescent, but the moon was on her back. I can't wait to see if the water really goes down the plughole the other way, the opposite to the northern hemisphere. It's warm, but not hot, and it's beautiful. Well it isn't, but anywhere terra firma after ten hours trapped at sixty thousand feet seems beautiful.

Ian Curtis and I then flew on to Victoria Falls to take a detour and here we are staying at the Elephant Hills Hotel, in the lap of luxury. The view of the Zambezi river basin is second to none, and the awesome spray rising from above the Victoria Falls can just be seen from my room. We've been told that at dawn and dusk the animals come out on the golf course, and there is a water hole between the last hole and the hotel itself where elephants and giraffes and all manner of creatures come down to drink. But the only elephants we saw were 12-inch high tee markers on the 18-hole golf course.

Superb buffet dinner – steaks like you would not believe. The meat just melts in the mouth. Feel sorry for Ian at this point as he is a veggie. He looks longingly at my plate but can't bring himself to sneak a bite – even when I promise not to tell anyone. I tell him how unfair it is that when you have a veggie over for a dinner party you have to make sure there's a vegetarian dish, but if you went to a vegetarian for dinner, they wouldn't cook a meat dish specially for you. He doesn't appreciate the logic. Ian then gets his own back by trying to convince me to do a bungy jump off the Victoria Falls bridge the next day. He actually believes it's quite normal to want to throw yourself off one of the tallest bridges in the world, and pay $90 for the privilege. People apparently come from all over the world to bungy off the Victoria Falls bridge. It's one of the highest ones you can do in the world.

It's the thing that the Falls are known for, Ian argues. What else is there to do there? I retort fairly lamely, 'Look at it.' He seems absolutely set on it himself, and I agree a compromise – a day of white water rafting down some of the biggest and fastest rapids that the mighty Zambezi river has to offer. We saw video footage at the airport of the rafting while we waited for our domestic connection and I must say it did look very exciting – careering at high speed down these gushing torrents of white spray. We book it for tomorrow plus a helicopter ride over the Falls themselves, but I know Ian is going to continue to work on me over the bungy – the answer is most categorically No.

Wednesday 2 July

Rafting absolutely fantastic. The Sheerwater Company organised a superb day – safe as houses – life jackets, helmets, paddles, lunatic instructors. Ten rafts with eight of us in each. To think they do that every day defies belief. At least you couldn't bring your work home with you. There was an instructor in each boat and they had names like 'Nelson' and 'Risky George'. Ours was called 'Lion King' and he was very big on Manchester United. The rapids all had names like 'The Washing Machine', 'Commercial Suicide', 'The Muncher', 'The Devil's Toilet Bowl', and 'Oblivion'. The guides-come-instructors described them as they came to each one – not the most confidence-inspiring of gestures, it has to be said.

ME So what's this next one called?

LION KING Oblivion.

ME Why's that?

LION KING You get a lot of 'Downtiming'.

ME What's 'Downtiming'?

LION KING When the raft flips and you go down – whirlpools and boils in the water hold you under.

ME Great. I'll look forward to that one then.

In the evening we have to replay the day again, because of course they've only gone and videoed the whole thing. And although once you've seen one raft struggling down one set of rapids with eight very silly blue helmets and life jackets bobbing up and down, you've seen them all, most of the rafting veterans seem very excited by their immortalisation on video. I suppose it provides a memory of the occasion and perhaps proof to their friends that they were silly enough to attempt it in the first place. They could even buy the videos and photographs at exorbitant prices. Ian and I bemoaned the commercialisation of it all.

Victoria Falls is now very big business. It's like a huge great natural theme park, and you've just got to think of another way of tapping into people's daredevilling, outward-bound spirit to make your own fortune. I come up with the idea of reinforced steel and glass barrels that you could climb into and have pushed over the edge of the Falls. It seems very sad in some ways that such a mighty natural phenomenon – it is one of the seven wonders of the world, after all – should have to bear the scars of such commercialisation: rafting, sightseeing cruises, aeroplane and helicopter flights, and, of course, bungying.

Ian found out this evening that he has been offered the part of 'Legs' Lane in the forthcoming film version of Andy McNab's book *Bravo Two Zero* – based on his experiences at the hands of the Iraqis in the Gulf War. McNab has also done the screen adaptation and Sean Bean will be playing the author. This is brilliant news for Ian, so the beers are on him tonight. And it also means that he'll be coming back to this part of the world again in August, as the film is being shot in South Africa for five weeks, with a week in England first.

Thursday 3 July

Don't know how to say this. There isn't any other way of saying this. I can only explain it by saying I had a temporary loss of sanity: I ended up doing the bungy jump. Still don't understand how Curtis persuaded me to do it. Suddenly at around midday I found that he had lured me over the Zambian border just 'to see the bridge and the falls from the Zambian side'. I'm sure that if one of the other boys had been there, like Tom or Danny, I would have veered towards sanity and not done it.

IAN You've got to do the bungy jump. Just think – when will you ever get the chance to come here again?

ME Ian, I'm coming back here in three weeks time with Miranda.

I hated every moment. Didn't get this 'buzz' people talk about. The only sensation I got felt like I was having a heart attack. The guys that run the bungy jump told me that they no longer get the buzz from simply jumping. They have to do increasingly more dangerous things to get the same adrenaline rush. It's become an addiction for most of them. One New Zealander with goatee down to his chest told me that his most recent achievement – I use the word 'achievement' loosely – was to do the jump from the bridge, but without any harness, because 'harnesses are for wimps anyway'. He simply held the rubber rope; it wasn't even attached around the feet.

I try to imagine this but my brain stops me. I've always suffered from a fear of heights. He then said that the real buzz came when the bungy became taut for the first time with his weight – because that was the moment at which he let go of the bungy and dropped the few feet into the waiting Zambezi. Silence fell over the conversation and I felt I no longer had anything in common with this cracked Kiwi. In some ways I feel jealous that he had that experience, that pleasure – that I've missed out. And Ian wanted to do it again straight away. How can two people have such vastly different experiences of the same thing? We're at completely different ends of the spectrum.

Had to buy the video of the jump to prove to myself in years to come that I didn't imagine the whole thing. Also to prove to Miranda that I did it. When I tell her what I've done, there's silence followed by her telling me to run it by her again as she thinks she misheard me, she thought I said I'd done a bungy jump. I say I have done a bungy jump and she reminds me I'm the father of a small child. I tell her that Abraham can now boast to his friends that his dad has done a bungy jump. M reminds me that Abraham can't actually speak yet, let alone boast to his friends. He could just about say 'bungy' she says, and 'stupid twit' will also be on her list to teach him in the next few days. At the moment, though, he does seem to have grasped that Daddy has gone away to work on a plane. Apparently, there's lots of pointing to the sky and 'Daddy, plane'. This fills me with terrible pangs of homesickness.

'Daddy helicopter as well,' I say to M. She's now totally confused. I explain that Ian and I also went up in a helicopter after the bungy jump to view the Victoria Falls from above. After returning from the Zambian side – to get to the bridge you have to cross the border into Zambia – we dashed up to the aerodrome and got in a four-seater helicopter. Quite frankly, although we were only over the Falls for 15 minutes, it was the highlight of the trip for me – far more buzz than bungy jumping, and in a different league to white water rafting. This was the ultimate. Only from above can you actually get the size and scale, the beauty and the uniqueness of it.

It was then a rush to the hotel, to pick up the bags and on to the airport and our flight back to Harare. Ian was due in Matare that evening for costume fittings and a meeting with the director, Roger Tucker. I was beginning to wonder whether Roger was a mythical figure. Who was Roger Tucker? Sounds like Roger Rabbit. Who framed Roger Tucker? Is he going to be a 'Rog', as opposed to a Roger?

Think I'm suffering from Bungius Jumpus Syndrome. Brain going off on uncontrollable tangents – comparable feeling to the same few bars of a song

Above: The magnificent Victoria Falls, as seen from the helicopter.

going round and round in your head interminably. Keep getting flashbacks to the jump. Snapshots in my brain of the moment after throwing myself off, then a second later falling, and another, falling, and my hands outstretched pathetically, trying to stop myself falling any further. Image of myself as a cartoon character. The wolf in 'Roadrunner' after he's gone running over the edge of a mountain and he suddenly realises and plummets.

I decide to stay in Harare for a couple more days. The Sheraton is very comfortable. This is the Zimbabwe base for cast and crew. I bump into Dermot – focus-puller Dermot – and armourer Rob and they have apparently been putting off the inevitable rendezvous in Mutare for as long as possible.

Dermot There's nothing there.
Me There's got to be something.
Dermot I'm telling you, there isn't.
Rob Apparently, it's like Stevenage, but even worse.

Friday 4 July

Spend most of today down town sorting out family holiday for when M and Abe come out and join me after I've finished filming. Surprised at how many skyscrapers actually litter the skyline. Harare is a bustling, commercial hub. A big and busy city.

For once I had a slight understanding of what it must be like for a black person in a mainly white domain. I was very much in the minority and I saw very few white faces. On another level, I also felt very aware of the history of the country and had a sense of the struggle that these people had undergone. Something just hung in the air for me. The legacy of apartheid through the old Colonial and Empire buildings that still remain was there, engrained in the bricks. Even nearly twenty years later, after independence. What must it be like in South Africa?

Mugabe isn't the liberal I assumed he was. He has made it clear recently, for example, that homosexuality is against the law here, and he has ruled with a rod of iron for the last eighteen years since independence.

There are three important things you need to know about President Mugabe:

1 He owns some very nice property in Switzerland.

2 His picture is everywhere, but I'm afraid it's a bit of a passport jobby.

3 Mugabe spelt backwards and spoken by a Yorkshire person would be 'E Ba Gum.'

BELOW: Me and James Cosmo with some of the local kids who lived near one of the African locations

THE TECHNICALITIES:

The focus puller

Dermot is a terrific focus puller, always calm, always there checking distances from lens to eyeball with his trusty tape measure. This is the old-fashioned type which surveyors always use and which needs to be wound up after the tape has been pulled out. Always talking American Football numbers to himself slightly under his breath – focal lengths – or to Madeleine on continuity who has to write them all down for reference. Does that mean that you can equate the focus puller on a film set with the quarter back on the American Football field? 'No Jonathan, I doubt it.'

Saturday 5 July

Have been taken under the wing of a British Airways cabin crew, Louise and Stuart, in Harare on a stopover. They mistake me for one of their pilots. I try and bluff it out, but finally the talk just gets too technical for me to keep up. Spent the afternoon working on the script with half of British Airways – by the pool. Later played tennis care of British Airways while working on the script. Had dinner with British Airways still working on the script. It was all go. No rest for the wicked. Some of the hardest work I've ever had to do on 'Soldier, Soldier'. It's a tough job, but hell, someone's got to do it.

Beginning to pick up the cabin crew jargon. After a day in the sun I'm beginning to look like one of them too. Spent a few hours this evening looking for a trolley to push. They certainly don't like the 'trolley dolly' jokes – wearing a bit thin now.

Wish I could just tell a joke and walk away. But have this terrible habit of enjoying it too much myself, and constantly re-visit. Smiles the first time turn to 'I'll punch him if he says that again' looks of disdain.

GLASWEGIAN BA STEWARD I'm afraid that joke really doesn't get any funnier. It wasn't actually that funny in the first place, but we thought it was polite to humour you.
(Silence)

ME You don't know a Fiona Bell do you? She plays my wife in the series, and she's from Glasgow.

Still he managed to get his own back by doing what tends to happen when I mention 'Soldier, Soldier':

FIRST RESPONSE 'Soldier, Soldier'? Really? You're in that are you? I've never watched it myself.

ME Well, ten million other people do.

SECOND RESPONSE Isn't that the series with them two lads? What's their names? Robson and Jerome. That's it.

ME They left a couple of years ago.

THIRD RESPONSE Really? Are you going to be releasing a single then?

ME No. A diary as a matter of fact.

That normally shuts them up. What I'd really like to do is get a card printed up with the three questions and answers written in huge capital letters and give it to people as soon as I'm introduced to them.

The Father, Son and Ryan Giggs

Sunday 6 July Episode 10

Met Annie, Helen, Peter Lancaster and Joan Murphy in the lobby of The Sheraton. I'm suffering badly from the effects of the malaria pills, feeling very sick and woozy; decided to stop taking them. Picked-up rest of the actors from the airport first thing. Chat to Peter (ideal casting: a bank manager), the financial controller, while we're waiting for the plane to land. He's been in the business for fifty years, and worked with a lot of the greats: Charlton Heston, Robert Mitchum, Tom Craig. Joan, the production accountant, thrusts a small brown paper envelope into my hand, saying, 'I expect you'll be glad to see those.'

I certainly was. This was my cash allowance for the week for evening meals and the like. I was flush again. Everyone who'd come off the plane had that 'jaded but getting a second wind' look that people have after travelling on a long haul flight. But it was a breath of fresh air to see familiar faces, and it was a joy to be able to bore them rigid with bungy tales and rafting scares.

We were supposed to fly to Mutare – which is in the Eastern Highlands, on the border with Mozambique – in a couple of small six-seater aircraft which Annie and Helen had organised. But the weather closed in, so we ended up having to make the trip by road. We'd been told that it's like the Scottish Highlands up there. All the boys travelled in one van except for Danny, who somehow found himself in the other van with Annie, Helen Flint (production manager), the accountants, and Lucy Cohu and Kate O'Malley.

During the four hour drive I read edited highlights of the diary to the boys, who all wanted to know what I've said about them. Jimmy Cosmo got out his duty-free whisky and we all took healthy nips so as not to offend Jimmy, and to stave off the boredom of the journey, or it could have been the boredom of me reading the diary, I was too drunk to remember exactly what the boys said.

Left: Kate O'Malley (Pte Stacey Butcher) joined us in Africa.

Jimmy decided he wants Gene Hackman to play him in the movie, and we all decided that Stan Ogden would have been a definitive Danny Cunningham. Although we're not so sure about Hilda Ogden as Kate O'Malley.

The battery for the laptop ran out so that spelled the end of the highlights. Instead, we stopped to expel the whiskey from our bladders and when we piled back into the van, Danny was waiting for us, having transferred himself from Annie's.

So off we went again and to help pass the time I asked the boys if they had got any special requests for inclusions in the diary. No one could think of anything in particular. We jokingly bemoaned the fact that it always seems to be the same whenever you ask people to come up with something specific like that, especially a bunch of guys. Why is it – in an argument – that women can always remember every incident, every minute detail of what their partner did or didn't do, but when the partner starts to plead his defence, and the woman asks him to name specific examples, he can't remember a single one? A book called *Men are from Mars, Women are from Venus* gets mentioned. Sounds about right.

Chris tells me that his mate Andy – Andy from Hankley – has had his baby. Well, not him exactly, but his partner. He'd come down again to play a part in episode 12 – he thought he was going to be playing 'Gary No Hair' the A-company Prince of Trivia, but in actual fact he ended up as 'Squaddie 2'. But his girlfriend's timing was immaculate – let's hope the conception wasn't. He finished on the Thursday, and she had the baby on the Saturday, but if he'd been playing 'Gary No Hair', he would have been working on the day that the baby came. Here's to little Owen Peter, weighing in at seven and a half pounds.

We all have a nip of whisky to wish him well.

One sad note – the boys tell me that Dave the rigger (ideal casting: anyone from Oasis) was involved in an accident falling off a ladder, and has back injuries. So we all have another nip of whisky to wish him well, too.

Chris starts complaining of 'flu symptoms, so out comes the whisky again.

Sunday evening – there is a welcoming do for all cast and crew now that everyone is marooned in Mutare. I meet Roger 'Rabbit' Tucker for the first time. He sounds South African or Zimbabwean, definitely Southern Hemispherish, and so I ask him what the film business is like over here. He shakes his head and says he doesn't know, he's from Bristol.

Edward Brett is the first AD out here, and has already been stuck in Mutare for five weeks, swamped with the recce-ing of locations and preparing for the King's Own Carlton cameras to land. Jamie Christopher, who is Edward's second, is nothing like how I imagined him to look going on what his voice sounded like from his phone calls to me in England and Harare. For some reason, I was expecting a tanned fortysomething, balding, Sheriff of Nottingham black beard, heavy St Christopher chain. Instead I see before me a twentysomething Viking.

Tuesday 8 July episode 10

Day off yesterday. Tried to confirm holiday through Becky (ideal casting: Kate Jackson, from 'Charlie's Angels'), Jamie's girlfriend. Decided I was wrong about the Viking (ideal casting: Bill Clinton – but he might be a bit busy saving the world at the moment, and he might not like the 'White Water' references from

Victoria Falls, so I reckon I'll have to ask Conor to get Brian Dennahey's agent on the phone).

Imagine a small mid-West town in the USA and you'd be somewhere near what the geography and the architecture is like here, but with little English details like red post boxes and the cars driving on the left. Went past a sign a few blocks away from The Holiday Inn that says 'Aggressive Undertakers' – that's their name. I wonder what that involves? 'Right. We've come early. And we want you NOW.'

Mutare is like a small Ohio farming town in 1964. Wide streets, grid system. Could be the location for 'Back to the Future'. The only place to eat other than the hotel is a steakhouse called The Black Steer, and if you eat there often enough, you're allowed to become a member of the Black Steer Frequent Dining Club. After ten meals you get a free one. But the sad bit is that it only costs about a fiver for a fantastic, huge juicy steak that melts in your mouth, so it's hardly costing an arm and a leg in the first place.

Starting to get to grips with the currency here. The mark-up in the hotel is enormous. A beer in a bar which costs 5 Zimbabwe dollars would cost you 12 in the Holiday Inn, or 18 in the Sheraton in Harare. The exchange rate is approximately 18 dollars to the pound. The extras are being paid about ten pounds a day, and they tell me that 180 Zim dollars a day is relatively good. The Zim dollar is reminiscent of Monopoly money. Lots of notes. Big ones like hundreds and fifties. And if you land on Mutare, you cannot pass go, you cannot collect two hundred dollars, and you have to go straight to jail.

Mutare is the ultimate 'miss a turn' town. Still, I've eaten more beef in the last week than in the whole of the last five years. More cloud and rain today – this really could be Scotland. Fancy coming all the way to Africa and it raining like this. Very little film so far to show we actually are in Africa – could easily be Hankley Common.

The air conditioning in the hotel is a nightmare. You can't turn it off. You can't turn it down. You can't make it warmer. I've resorted to covering mine with a towel to prevent hypothermia of an evening and sleeping in layers is advisable. Everyone coming down with colds as a result. Chris Gascoyne really not very well at all.

The episode in Africa revolves around the King's Own Fusiliers coming to the fictional state of Zokindi to provide humanitarian assistance to the local people caught up in a bitter civil war. Today we filmed the ambush sequence, where a small detachment of the fusiliers has been assigned to escort the rebel leader to the refugee camp. It's a highly dangerous operation as much of the territory between the rebels and the camp is controlled by the government's forces, and inevitably, they are ambushed by a well-trained group of mercenaries. It isn't actually explicit-

BEHIND-THE-SCENES:

The first showing

The production office has taken over a whole suite at the hotel and this evening after work we all piled into one of the rooms to watch a video that Annie has brought with her of episode 1. The show is excellent. The movie paid off. Still, it's never wise to second-guess the audience or the critics, so I'll wait with interest to see how the series does. We will, of course, be up against it again with the European football, every other week. However, the viewing figures that the TV companies get the day after the programme has been shown are able to take into account all those people who've recorded 'Soldier, Soldier' on their videos. How this is technologically possible I do not know.

After the showing of episode 1, we put on the video of our far more dramatic bungy jumps. Suddenly, I was right back there, re-living the whole experience. My heart started pounding again, and it looked even worse on screen. It's horrible seeing the moments when I knew I was unhappy or panicking. This is in stark contrast to that nutter Curtis who has a broad manic grin from ear to ear. The rest of the audience were equally horrified, and couldn't quite believe that we'd done it, having actually now seen the height and the drop. I turned round and caught all their faces staring with knotted brows, and that strange constipated look of imagined pain as they were all visualising their own 'could I or couldn't I do that' moment. Indulged myself in moment of reflected bravery.

ly stated that the mercenaries are working for the government, but I've taken it as read that they are. They are commanded by Colonel Walker (Alex Norton), and coincidentally Mark Hobbs, ex-King's Own, has recently joined Walker's merry band. I wonder what are the chances of that actually happening?

Roger decided not to shoot anything of the actual ambush, preferring to make a jump cut from Chris McCleod climbing down from the back of the leading Land Rover to help a mother and her child, who are acting as a decoy for the mercenaries, to a shot of Chris's hands in the air and a gun at his head.

While I was standing with my hands in the air, I noticed that the second of the two cameras being used on the shot was accidentally still turning over, when they were both supposed to have stopped. I only knew this because if you look down the lens of a camera that is still running, you can see the shutter flickering.

What it will have captured, however, is me noticing the flickering and then striding off through the undergrowth towards the camera. As I did so, I brushed past a seemingly innocuous, tall, bright green plant, which left some fine hairs on the tops of my trousers. Well, suddenly it felt like I'd been stung by about ten wasps on each thigh. And several huge welts came up immediately. I think the locals, playing mercenaries, must have been confused, because I certainly didn't grin and bear the pain like a good soldier. I was shouting for a nurse and running around with my trousers round my ankles. The nurse asked me if I wanted to go somewhere a bit more private for her to rub the antiseptic cream on my thighs, but I was desperate and declined. The way I was feeling, they could have filmed the whole thing, just as long as they got that stuff on as quickly as possible to get rid of the pain.

My thighs had now turned bright red, and I was getting all worked up about the fact that no one had said anything to do with the dangers of the local flora and fauna. Suddenly, everyone wanders over to examine these long and exotic looking monsters. They nod and come over to tell me how dangerous and painful they can be. I tell them I know. Next time I notice the camera still running, I think I'll just work on my own close-up, until someone else realises what's happened.

Wednesday 9 July episode 10

Counselling required because there are no doughnuts out here. I repeat – there are no doughnuts here. This is a doughnut-free zone. Still haven't totally taken in the implications of that. I got very excited at one point when the words 'Danish pastry' were mentioned, but I think they've got the wrong end of the stick with that one. Their idea of a Danish pastry is more like a cross between a scone and an angel cake – nothing Danish about that.

Starting to get into irritating habit of leaping up from my desk or jumping off the bed when I hear voices coming down the corridor and padding down the room to the spy hole in the door to see whoever it is. I obviously don't want to think I'm missing out on anything. Must stop this. Last night I was up and down like a yo-yo. I didn't even know or see half the people that came past. But now getting strange buzz that they don't know that I'm looking at them through the spyhole.

Today, Chris Gascoyne did an excellent trick on Keith, from wardrobe. Keith needed to ring Chris to speak to him quite urgently, something to do with

RIGHT: Edward Brett, first AD, was already looking like something from 'Out of Africa' by the time we arrived.

his costume and needing him to come for a fitting. So he rang down to reception to get Chris's room number, then straightaway dialled it. Only every time he thought he was getting through to Chris's room, a voice would say 'Hello, reception'. After this happened three times, Keith started to get a bit hot under the collar. So, he rang reception again and started to give the guy a right old earhole of grief, telling him that every time he dialled Mr Gascoyne's room number he was getting reception, and 'what the hell was going on?' The guy was very apologetic and said he didn't know what the problem could be other than it was Keith dialling the wrong number. He said he would connect Keith personally, and a few moments later there was a ringing tone as he waited for Chris to pick up the phone. But, again, when the voice answered he said, 'Hello, reception.'

KEITH Call this a hotel. What the hell's going on here? I urgently need to speak to Mr Gascoyne in room number 212. This really isn't good enough. I keep trying the number, and I know I'm dialling the correct number, so something is definitely wrong with this phone.

CHRIS (in his best Zimbabwean accent) Mr Gascoyne has decided to move to another hotel.

KEITH (huge sigh) Another hotel? Which hotel? Is it nearby. I must know which hotel he has moved to.

CHRIS Keith. Keith. Calm down. It's me. I was just having a laugh.

KEITH I can't believe it. I've been trying to get hold of you for the last ten minutes.

CHRIS I know.

KEITH What?

CHRIS Hello, reception.
(Silence)

KEITH You bastard.

Today, they blew up one of the aid trucks at the air strip. One of the young lads, Matthew, who was playing a fusilier extra, fell over as we ran to take cover from the incoming fire. I nearly fell over him, and when he got up I noticed that he had left half the skin covering his elbow on the gravelly tarmac, and that he'd got a London accent.

ME Where are you from?

MATTHEW Southeast London.

ME Where exactly?

MATTHEW Brockley.

ME You're joking. I was brought up in Eltham. My mother still lives there. Where did you go to school?

MATTHEW Askes

ME No. My mother teaches in the Askes girls' school.

It's a very odd feeling when you meet someone on the other side of the world that you suddenly find out shares your own geography and history. Matthew is out in Zimbabwe teaching primary school children before he goes off to university in England. And he's picking up a bit of extra cash as an extra in 'Soldier, Soldier'. I then discover through him that there are other Brits doing this as well. They are all a nice bunch of guys, especially Ian, who's been out here for four years, teaching children and organising projects. The language spoken in this area is called Shona, and Ian is fluent in it, much to the surprise of the locals who don't know him. Taken on Conor today as my 'Ideal casting' assistant. He has had a brainwave for James Cosmo. We will now be making an offer to Nick Nolte first thing in the morning.

Thursday 10 July episode 10

This afternoon I went to get photos developed. Almost twice the price it is in England.

But there are some real beauties of the Victoria Falls from the helicopter. I even managed to get a shot of the rainbow that can always be seen from a particular angle over the Falls when the sun is out. I'd forgotten there were a couple of photos of Abraham on the film, from the day before I left. He'd gone into our bedroom and slipped my trainers on over his own shoes, and shuffled out into the kitchen to show us. He looks so beautiful and I'm so proud of him. And it's reassuring to think he looks so happy in the photo – with his Babar sweatshirt and very grown-up jeans.

Ian and Alex went on a horseback safari. Saw a herd of zebra. Played with a baby lion cub. They were saying that it's quite common for families to rear a lion cub.

Dinner at the Black Steer. Discussed re-birthing with Ben, Alex and Ian. Sounds interesting. I'll have to investigate when I get home.

Friday 11 July episode 10

Simon Bray is the camera operator on this episode and I deduced from his long-sleeved T-shirt today – which says 'Common As Muck 2' on it – that he was the camera operator on that as well. These days, all the cast and crew of TV dramas and series are wearing some piece of clothing which has emblazoned on it, either subtly – or sometimes quite garishly – the name of that production. It's the in-thing to wear as a member of the crew. It's a sort of unofficial hierarchical uniform, which tells you straight away whether the person you are talking to has done movies, or just TV, etc. Baseball caps are a favourite, so too now are fleeces (woolly anoraks) which are more or less obligatory for an assistant director upwards, and which say straight away that this person has worked on a night shoot. Puffa jackets are still up there as well, along with sweatshirts – and I quite liked Pip Torrens' donkey jacket with 'Bodyguards' written like an armband on one sleeve. I wonder if anyone has thought of 'Soldier, Soldier' underwear? But having said that, there wouldn't be any point in putting the logo on a pair of camouflage knickers or boxer shorts, unless you decided to wear them over your trousers.

Simon (ideal casting: Jeff Goldblum – I was advised by Simon that getting Jeff was the price I had to pay for him not making me look hideous on film) told a story about filming 'Indiana Jones' at Pinewood. They built an eight-foot deep tank covering the whole of a sound stage, and put over a thousand real snakes and five thousand plastic ones in it for the famous scene where Jones (Harrison Ford) pushes over the statue in the tomb. Today, snakes still keep cropping up all over the place at Pinewood because they failed to recover all the snakes from that infamous tank at the time.

No13 Solut
N56kg

Chris is still not well. It's been nearly a week, and I'm worried that his lasting impression of being in Africa is of being ill. I still have to pinch myself sometimes, just to remind myself that I'm in Africa. I'm actually in Africa. What must it have been like when Livingstone and his huge party of bearers chopped a path out of jungle and reached Victoria Falls? He must have wanted to tell the whole world straight away that he'd found them.

In the mini bus, on the way back from filming, it suddenly became clear why Tom Craig had worn his special new Sheffield Wednesday shirt. He came up to me as we were getting on it, and in a conspiratorial 'I can get you some very good gear' manner and tone of voice, asked me if I'd take his picture. I said, of course, and started trying to take my camera out. He said, 'No, not now. On the trip back.'

He wanted to stop on the way. I was surprised because I hadn't put Tom down as the type to have noticed a nice view at which to stop and have a picture taken. Had he found a place where the elephants came out?

TOM Not exactly. But you are close about the wildlife

Half an hour later, just as I was dozing, the word 'stop' boomed out over the bus, and Tom pointed to a sign by the side of the road. I did not understand what on earth was going on.

TOM I want my picture taken standing by that sign.

ME Why do you want your picture taken by that sign?

TOM Look at it. Go on look at it. What do you see?

ME The Wise Owl Motel.

Tom So?

Me I don't know. You want to go and stay there?

Tom NO. Owls, Jon. Owls.

Me What are you talking about?

Tom Sheffield Wednesday are the Owls. This is going in the Fanzine above the caption: 'Owls on tour in Zimbabwe.'

What I hadn't realised was that this was a special occasion. This was an event that warranted the wearing of the prized new Wednesday shirt.

ABOVE: Sheffield Wednesday fan on tour: Zimbabwe, July '97

Saturday 12 July episode 10

6.15am pick up from the Holiday Inn. Forty-five minute drive to the location – the mercenary camp. It's an incredible place. An old tobacco hanging warehouse made of brick. The cream paint has long since faded, or else someone has spent one hell of a long time distressing the whole place. There is a complex wooden framework structure inside the brick shell. It's been dressed by the designer and set decorator with all manner of hammocks and living areas, carefully balanced tables, old car seats, mosquito nets, all blending into the log structure. It resembles Colonel Kurtz's camp in 'Apocalypse Now'. This explains why Alex has been asking for a body double for his scenes as Colonel Walker

LEFT: Filming the explosion at the air strip.

– because Brando had to have one as Colonel Kurtz. Brando had put on so much weight before filming that Coppola could only get away with shooting him in semi-darkness. In the end it was incredibly effective, as one of the lasting and most haunting images of the film was the scene between Brando and Martin Sheen. Will Alex's stuff with Ian, who has joined the mercenaries, be equally memorable and haunting?!

It really does look like Billy Smart's Circus has come to town. There are marquees and tents and generators and vehicles everywhere. All the actors are changing in a row of tents – which is worrying because one knows what people say about both actors and rows of tents. And the actors' camp, as it's called, looks like a cross between a safari stop-over and a medieval jousting tournament. Among the idiosyncracies of the specially customised make-up wagon is this particular joy. When you turn on the tap in the sink, the water spurts out like it is being ejaculated; the vibration of the pump then causes the flies who are sleeping on the shelf above to oscillate up and down in time with the throb of the pump. It looks like their whole bodies are hiccupping in time. Poor Chris Howard is having a tough time with the light. (But one piece of good news – instead of Kermit the Frog, Dustin Hoffman has said he will think about the Chris Howard role.)

The sun is in and out like a yo-yo. It's worse than England. We're having four seasons in a day as well, which is proving fairly tricky with the whole production. There's hundreds of extras every day. Sarah Ryan (ideal casting: Nicole Kidman) and Keith (Kevin Bacon) in wardrobe, are having to sort out hundreds of costumes every day and they are long days, starting at 6am and not finishing until early evening, and then they have to stay even longer to put costumes away, clear things up.

BEHIND-THE-SCENES:

Script changes?

Today we are filming scenes of the King's Own Fusiliers arriving in Zokindi in the back of the transport aircraft, and on the tarmac. Bit of a jittery moment when Roger tried to capture a line on celluloid that Chris Gascoyne just didn't like. It wasn't even that it was a bit offensive, it just was quite a poor gag. Bailey is supposed to walk past the line of Fusiliers on the tarmac, and Rossi, played by Gascoyne, has his face pointing straight up to the sun with his eyes closed, trying to catch some rays. In the end, Tom thought of something much funnier than the original line.

BAILEY Planning on acquiring a sun tan Rossi?

ROSSI Yes, Ma'am. You wait till you see me in my thong.

And then the next time you see him, after Sgt McCleod has bollocked him, he is digging the latrines. And we thought carrying on from that, McCleod would make Rossi dig the latrines in just this thong and his boots. But we had the feeling that there wasn't even any point in mentioning that idea.

Had relaxing reiki massage from Alex, who's playing one of the fusilier extras. I lay on a rock overlooking the tobacco hanging mercenary camp. He's very Zen and tells me that reiki is all about unlocking the flow of energy from certain points in the body. Sounded good to me. He'd just come back from spending three months in Scotland at a Highland retreat, which is more of a community where all kinds of alternative therapies and medicines are practised and taught. While I had my massage, just metres away on the same bit of rock which spectacularly overlooked a picture-book image of an African vista, Alex and Ian played the scene where Walker tells Hobbs that it's up to him to get rid of not only the rebel leader, but the King's Own escort as well.

Over lunch, Chris Gascoyne told a great story about his tattoos. One of them is filled in but originally, when he went to have it done, he wanted his name 'Chris' tattooed in the middle. He had to go and have it done in his lunch break, but unfortunately also at lunch was the tattooist himself. His mate was holding the fort until the tattooist returned, and said with considerable confidence that he could do the tattoo that Chris had picked out, 'No problem.' What he didn't tell Chris was that he'd never attempted writing words before.

Initially, all went well as the man worked round the pattern on Chris's arm. Then suddenly he uttered the immortal phrase, now scarred on Chris's brain:

TATTOO APPRENTICE Oops youth, I've bollocksed.

CHRIS (through the beads of sweated pain) What is it?

TATTOO APPRENTICE I'm afraid I've spelt Chris wrong. I've missed out the 'R'.

CHRIS Eh? You're joking?

TATTOO APPRENTICE I'll try and have another go at it.

To Chris's horror the man had indeed forgotten the 'R', and he was now making a bad job worse. Finally, through clenched teeth and increasingly unbearable pain, he told the 'incompetent' to fill the whole thing in. But, very vaguely, you can still pick out the letters underneath. So, I'm afraid that from now on, Chris will have to be referred to as 'Chis' – 'Chis' Gascoyne. And if this isn't enough, 'Chis' then rolls up his combat trousers and shows the whole table his shin. On it can just be seen, in faded black ink, a three inch arrow, pointing to his other leg.

ME Why have you got an arrow tattooed on your shin?

CHIS When I was at school everyone was doing it themselves – and I fancied having these anchors. But it got too painful, so I ended up with just one.

ME But that's not an anchor 'Chis' – that's an arrow.

CHIS I know. Pathetic isn't it.

It seemed to go dark at about half-past two in the afternoon. Fortunately, we'd moved inside one of the smaller warehouses – where the rebel leader and his escort are being held hostage. The fusiliers, as the escort, are getting increasingly more frustrated, and it comes near to blows when Walker and Hobbs come for Major Bailey, obviously with the intention of having their grubby way with her. Chris McCleod tries to intervene, but Bailey stops him with a forceful 'No, Sgt McCleod.' She offers herself up as a sacrifice, and walks off with them, spitting in Hobbs's face as she passes him. Dramatic stuff all right.

The trouble was that by about four o'clock we'd started to lose the plot. We were getting a bit hysterical. It had been a long long day and the schedule was bearing out our reason for hysteria. There were far too many scenes and set-ups to get in today. And as the light as well as the rain had gone so early, we couldn't come round and do the reverses (see box, left).

The final scene of the day was Chris McCleod getting a rifle butt in the back for having a go at a mercenary and pinning him up against the wall, as the escort was rounded up in the warehouse. We were pushed and prodded outside until we were up against the wall, waiting for the firing squad. The butt in Chris's back looked terribly painful, and one of the mercenaries who was watching the scene from outside the barn told his friend to be more careful with me as it looked like he was causing me terrible pain. But the guy told his friend that I was acting. I was also wearing a bloody great pad to stop me feeling anything.

Diary is really taking its toll now. I come back of an

THE TECHNICALITES:

Filming reverses

The dismal lighting meant that while the point of view of Walker and Hobbs as they were bursting into the warehouse where we were being held could be shot, the camera couldn't then come round and show our POV of the same event. The light and the rain outside would not match any of the other preceding exterior shots such as those of us being herded into the building.

evening, bath, then write the diary for an hour or so. I consume a room service cheese burger or visit The Black Steer, then bed at eleven-thirty. But there's only a few days left now, and I think I'm going to miss this evening ritual. Tonight I took a night off, and most of us went to the in-place to go to on a Saturday night in Mutare, 'The Place'. We danced the night away, and played pool for 12p a game. It could have been a 'Soldier, Soldier' party, as we were more or less the only ones in there until it started filling up at about 1am.

There was one strange and ugly series of incidents concerning a local guy, who looked like a Norwegian garden gnome with glasses. He took one look at Lucy, and started following her around and kneeling down in front of her. It was actually incredibly funny for about the first 15 minutes, because Danny and Chris kept stepping in between the gnome and Lucy, to protect her. But once the joke wore off it started to get quite sinister, and then just boring as it was affecting our evening. This guy just wouldn't leave her alone. He kept giving Chris, or whoever it was standing in front of him, his glasses, obviously inviting them to have a go at him. He even tried to buy drinks for everyone, but I'm afraid by then, no one was in the slightest bit interested in drinking with him. The only worry was that he might have a large hunting rifle in the back of his pick-up truck outside, and once he'd been slung out, he'd go back and get it. We decided to call it a night at about half-two.

Sunday 13 July episode 10

Today we went to the tobacco warehouse location to do a fight and stunt rehearsal organised by Jason White, the stunt co-ordinator. So no day off. We left at elevenish, got there at twelve, worked till three and then drove the hour or so back to the hotel. Robin Cope is also once again with us, as is Rob (ideal casting: Kevin Spacey), the armourer. Rob isn't just a gun doctor – he's a gun heart and lungs specialist, and brain surgeon all rolled into one. I'm glad he's on our side. I always find being around guns quite dangerous and scary, but Rob is so passionate about what he does that he manages to communicate a real sense of trust and safety that I've not experienced before.

Above: Two of the 'mercenaries': if you want a game of darts, you will have to fight us for it. Left: Only acting! McCleod is dragged out of the warehouse by the guards after hearing how much his holiday in Mauritius will cost.

Monday 14 July episode 10

Jason's lovely wife Abbi (ideal casting: Farrah Fawcett to Jason's Lee Majors) is also out here, doubling for Kate and Lucy in various stunts. There aren't many female stunt performers, but the few that are good, tend to work all the time. On the way to the location, Abbi talks about the hot springs that she's just visited – which are less than an hour's drive away. Sounds blissful. Think I'll pay a visit next weekend. Maybe even stay the night. I ask Jason and Abbi what it's like being married and both stunt performers. What's breakfast like? Does Abbi jump from the top of the stairs, while Jason sets fire to the toast? What on earth

RIGHT: A pearl amongst swine? Lucy Cohu, in glamourous mode, is joined by the boys (Ian Curtis, Danny Cunningham and Chris Gascoyne).

must their young son Marcus – who's out with them here in Mutare – think?

Abbi asks about the bungy. I knew she would. She's thinking of doing it. What do I say? Where do I begin?

They are now planning on using two and maybe even three cameras on most of the scenes at this location next week as they nearly all have a stunt in them. I can quite easily see us going over time at this location. I don't think three days is going to be enough time to get all the scenes and all the stunts done.

Most of the boys went and did the 'Smoker's Workout' at the gym when we got back. I was far more sensible and did the 'Steakeater's Workout' in the Black Steer. That free meal is getting closer and closer. Spoke to M and Abe today. Feeling very homesick whenever I speak to them. It's OK when I'm busy, but just talking to them, hearing their voices, is almost too much. Abe sounds too grown up.

Today Cliff Kent is with us once again. He's flown out to take more publicity stills for Carlton. This morning he is also doing a pre-arranged photo shoot of Lucy in various wonderful evening dresses by Frank Usher, Ben de Lisi and Catherine Walker. Lucy shows me the Polaroids at lunch, and she looks absolutely fantastic.

I cannot believe what has happened to my jeans after they have have come back from the laundry service. I'll never be able to wear them again. I nearly cut myself on the creases that have been made down the front of the legs. It's happened to everyone. There was a palpable wave of group mourning as we each opened our brown paper bags, examined the neatly folded clean clothes, and gasped in horror at the abominable destruction that has been visited on sixty pairs of Levis.

Keith from wardrobe was so disturbed and perturbed that this sort of cruelty still goes on to jeans in captivity, that he drew a diagram for the laundry service people for future reference. On a piece of paper he drew two pairs of trousers. On one pair there were creases down the front and he wrote in oversized and angry capitals 'Uncool'. And on the other pair there were no creases and the word 'Cool'. All he has to do is wait and see what happens on Thursday when another attempt is made to murder northern hemisphere fashion.

The make-up girls we've inherited for the African leg of this job are brilliant. Rob the armourer seems to know all the slang names for the make-up girls, names like: 'Slap dragons', 'Married member of the face police', 'Witches of Cyclax' and 'The piranha tank.' But, as Carol the team leader (ideal casting: Jamie Lee Curtis), says, 'Be careful sunshine, your appearance is in our hands.' Where do all these names come from? And why? Why pick on the make-up department?

The other make-up girls, Sian (ideal casting: Jennifer Jason Leigh) and Sue (Yvonne Goolagong), who's South African, are busy deciding what their code phrase is going to be for when things are not going too well. In the end, they decide on, 'The maracas are in the deep freeze', and any cock-ups are to be blamed on the altitude. Just at that moment, Edward Brett comes over on the walkie talkie:

'It's official. It's a f***-up', sounding reminiscent of the phrase from NASA, 'This is Mission Control, we have a situation here'. There was too much scheduled for today. The script is divided into eighths of a page, and although we were only down to do about a page on the schedule, this actually translated into five or six stunts, each one requiring a considerable amount of time to set-up to be safe. Squibs on walls for bullets, fire balls, mercenaries diving out of the way of a jeep.

After seeing Edward in his safari hat and tribal chief's walking stick, I've decided to consult a ouija board to see if we can get Stewart Granger to play him.

Sue seems to have come up with a fairly plausible explanation for the 'honey wagon' mystery. When I originally told her about my quest to discover the 'honey wagon' truth, she immediately became a disciple. And she took over from me, quizzing the crew for the Holy Grail of knowledge – that ultimate film terminology secret. It was Chris Howard who provided the most appropriate answer to date. It was quite obvious really. Isn't it always? When the thing is emptied at the end of the day, apparently, the mixture that runs out is supposed to resemble honey – in texture and colour. HOW DISGUSTING.

Wednesday 16 July episode 10

Tempers starting to fray. Only a few days left, and the schedule is looking extraordinarily tight. Palpable atmosphere. You could knife it in the back.

Riot scene at refugee camp with the King's Own holding off frantic, starving mob is difficult to shoot – in more ways than one. Technically, it's difficult, co-ordinating the 450 extras, all going for it like there was no tomorrow, but much harder than that is the fact that a lot of them probably know all too well what it's like to be in that position.

Robert Mitchum used to divide his scripts into 'AR' and 'NAR' (Acting Required, and No Acting Required), and so it was here – this was a definite 'NAR' scene. It was genuinely very scary watching these lovely and friendly people suddenly becoming a hysterical mob. You couldn't get extras back home to react with the passion that these people bring to the job. They were climbing all over the supplies truck, as we pushed and pulled them off. You really felt the stakes were high. And I immediately thought what the hell would it be like if this was for real.

As I jumped down from the cab of the lorry, the door was pushed back on me and I only just managed to pull my hand out before getting it crushed in the door. As it was, I ended up with a small but painful gash on the palm of my hand. Lots of blood, though, so I got a decent dose of sympathy.

The local guys who have been taken on as crew – drivers, runners, riggers, assistant directors, etc. – are all very friendly – all guys. It's a very male dominated society still. The women's place is still very much in the kitchen, in the bedroom, and in the wrong. What Zimbabwean women there are working on the show are either in the kitchen or in the office. One of my favourites is Rosie 'The Keeper of the Tea' (ideal casting: Whoopi Goldberg). Whereas in England, you have to fend for yourself, over here, we have the luxury of Rosie, who keeps us all supplied.

GMTV out with us for the next few days and some other journalists organised by Nick (the head of Stills at Carlton) and Shari-Jane (ideal casting: Lori Anderson), from the publicity dept. GMTV are going to do a three morning special when the series comes out in September – behind the scenes, etc. They like the idea of the diary, and would like me to go on as a guest – I'll have to think about that one. They want to show a bit of footage of the bungee jump (so maybe the public will be conned into thinking I'm a macho dare devil, and I'll start going up for all those Jean Claude Van Damme roles. No, maybe not).

Lunch yesterday with Nthati (ideal casting: Robin Givens - the ex-Mrs Mike Tyson) who plays Lilian. By some extraordinary coincidence not only do the King's Own Fusiliers face their old friend and comrade Mark Hobbs, but also

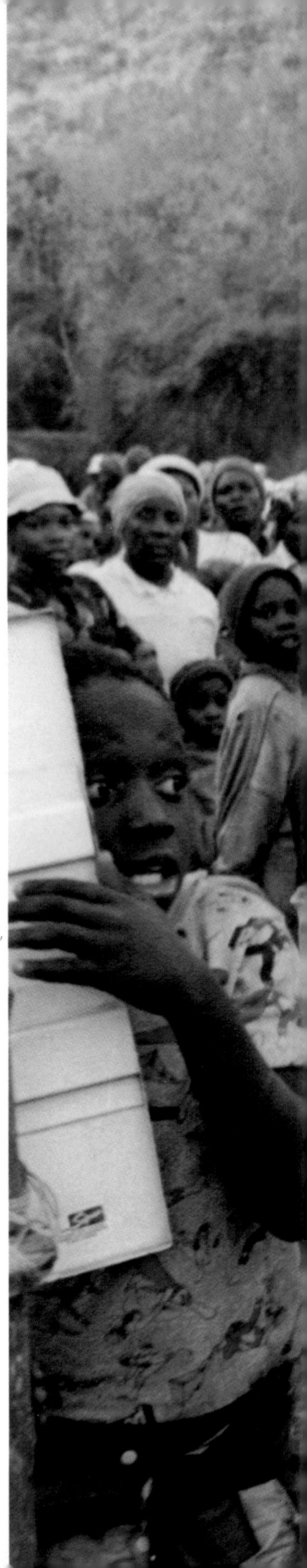

RIGHT: Jeremy (Ben Nealon) and Lilian (Nthati Moshesh) in Zokindi. 'Of all the refugee camps in all the world, you have to walk into mine.'

Forsythe's ex-wife happens to be working in the particular refugee camp that they have been sent to – even though she's from South Africa. It's lovely to see Nthati again. She looks as radiant and beautiful as she did last year. And I think she even remembers me. If she didn't, she certainly put on a convincing enough display when I bumped into her in the make-up lorry.

Thursday 17 July episode 10

The end is nigh. Mixture of sadness, relief, tiredness, anticipation, unemployment. Jimmy Cosmo is now Kirk Douglas – it's official. On the ideal casting front, I'm worried that I might be usurped by Kenneth Branagh who would want to direct and act in the movie of the making of the series. And now nearly three weeks after arriving in Africa, due to my excessive beef intake, I think it might be more appropriate if the ideal casting director approaches Orson Welles to play me.

I can feel the rumblings of the publicity machine as it grinds into action. First I was interviewed by GMTV in a field, with laptop on a table – very 'Out Of Africaish'. I've not once sat in a field to write my diary – but hey, it looks like a nice shot. 'The Big Breakfast' also came out to the set in Britain. I did it last year, live, on a ship moored off Bournemouth Pier. And I'm sure there will be a lot more besides GMTV's three day special. You get quite an insight into that whole media circus doing something as popular as 'Soldier, Soldier'.

Talked and played with some of the local kids. You just want to pick them up and take them home with you. They don't beg for money – they only want pens and books. I'm off to the stationers at the weekend to stock up with pens and pencils, crayons and paper to give them, and this is shortly to be followed by the arrival of M and Abe. Rejoice.

This diary is being sent back to England now. So that, basically, is it – 'Soldier, Soldier', the series, as seen from my lowly, but unique, perspective. I hope I haven't offended anyone too much who reads this.

'Once upon a time, in a land far away...'